Behind the Controversy: Legal and Political Issues of the U.S. Guantanamo Naval Base

ROBERTO MIGUEL RODRIGUEZ

Copyright Page

TITLE: Behind the Controversy: Legal and Political Issues of the U.S. Guantanamo Naval Base

1ST Edition

Behind the Controversy: Legal and Political Issues of the U.S. Guantanamo Naval Base

By Roberto Miguel Rodriguez

Chapter 1: The History of the U.S. Naval Base in Guantanamo, Cuba and its Importance in U.S.-Cuba Relations

The Establishment and Early History of the U.S. Naval Base in Guantanamo Bay, Cuba

Introduction:

The U.S. Naval Base in Guantanamo Bay, Cuba holds a unique place in the history of U.S.-Cuba relations. This subchapter explores the establishment and early history of the naval base, shedding light on its significance during different periods and its impact on the region. From its formation during the Spanish-American War to its role in the Cold War, the base has been at the center of numerous legal, political, economic, and human rights controversies. Examining its past helps us understand its present and offers insights into its potential future impact on U.S.-Cuba relations.

The Spanish-American War and the Birth of Guantanamo Naval Base:

The Spanish-American War of 1898 marked a turning point in Cuba's history, and it was during this conflict that the U.S. established the naval base in Guantanamo Bay. The strategic location of the bay, its natural harbor, and its proximity to the United States made it an ideal choice for a naval base. The U.S. Navy quickly recognized its potential as a refueling station and a means to protect American interests in the Caribbean.

The Cold War Era and the Guantanamo Naval Base:

During the Cold War, the Guantanamo Naval Base played a crucial role in U.S.-Cuba relations. As tensions between the United States and the

Soviet Union escalated, the base became a key outpost for monitoring Soviet activities in the region. It also served as a launching pad for intelligence gathering and counterterrorism efforts.

Legal and Political Controversies:

The Guantanamo Naval Base has been a subject of legal and political controversies. The lease agreement between the United States and Cuba has been a contentious issue, with Cuba arguing that it was signed under duress. The detention facilities established at the base for suspected terrorists have also sparked international criticism and raised questions about human rights and international law.

Economic Impact on the Local Cuban Community:

The naval base has had a significant economic impact on the local Cuban community. The base has provided employment opportunities for Cubans and has contributed to the local economy through trade and service industries. However, it has also created a dependence on the base, leaving the community vulnerable to fluctuations in U.S.-Cuba relations.

Conclusion:

The establishment and early history of the U.S. Naval Base in Guantanamo Bay, Cuba, have shaped its role in U.S.-Cuba relations. From its origins during the Spanish-American War to its significance in the Cold War, the base has been a site of both cooperation and contention. Its legal, political, economic, and human rights controversies have attracted international attention. Understanding the base's historical context is crucial for diplomats and historians seeking to comprehend its current impact and predict its future implications on U.S.-Cuba relations.

The strategic location of Guantanamo Bay

The U.S. Naval Base in Guantanamo Bay, Cuba holds a strategic location that has played a pivotal role in shaping U.S.-Cuba relations throughout history. Situated on the southeastern coast of Cuba, this naval base has proved instrumental in American military and political endeavors in the region.

The establishment of the Guantanamo Naval Base dates back to 1903, when the United States and Cuba signed the Cuban-American Treaty. This agreement granted the U.S. a perpetual lease on the area, ensuring its continued presence in the region. The base's close proximity to the Caribbean Sea and the Panama Canal made it an ideal location for American naval operations and surveillance.

During the Spanish-American War in 1898, the Guantanamo Naval Base played a crucial role. American forces used the base as a staging point for their operations, allowing them to quickly respond to Spanish threats in the region. This successful deployment cemented the base's importance in U.S.-Cuba relations and set the stage for its future significance.

Throughout the Cold War, the Guantanamo Naval Base gained further prominence. As tensions between the United States and the Soviet Union escalated, the base served as a critical intelligence gathering hub, monitoring Soviet activities in the region. It also provided a strategic location for American counterterrorism efforts, particularly during the Cuban Missile Crisis in 1962.

However, the Guantanamo Naval Base has not been without controversy. Its legal and political controversies have sparked global attention and debate. The detention facility established in 2002 to hold suspected terrorists has drawn criticism for its human rights implications and violation of international law.

Beyond its military and political significance, the Guantanamo Naval Base has had an economic impact on the local Cuban community. The presence of American military personnel and their families has created employment opportunities and stimulated the local economy.

Looking to the future, the Guantanamo Naval Base holds potential to influence U.S.-Cuba relations. As diplomatic efforts continue to evolve, the base's future remains uncertain. Its fate will undoubtedly impact the ongoing quest for democracy and stability in Cuba, as well as the broader relationship between the two nations.

In conclusion, the strategic location of the Guantanamo Naval Base has shaped the course of U.S.-Cuba relations. From its establishment to its role in major conflicts, this naval base has been at the center of historical and political developments. As diplomats and historians explore its multifaceted significance, it becomes evident that the Guantanamo Naval Base is not just a military facility, but a symbol of complex and evolving relations between two nations.

The negotiations between the U.S. and Cuba for the establishment of the naval base

The negotiations between the U.S. and Cuba for the establishment of the naval base in Guantanamo Bay are a crucial chapter in the history of U.S.-Cuba relations. These negotiations, which took place in the early 20th century, shaped the course of the U.S. Naval Base in Guantanamo and its significance in the geopolitical landscape.

The establishment and early history of the U.S. Naval Base in Guantanamo Bay were marked by complex negotiations between the two countries. In 1903, the U.S. and Cuba signed the Cuban-American Treaty, which granted the U.S. the right to establish a naval base in Guantanamo Bay. The negotiations leading up to this treaty were a delicate balance of diplomatic maneuvering and strategic considerations.

The role of the Guantanamo Naval Base in the Spanish-American War further solidified its importance in U.S.-Cuba relations. During the war, the base served as a strategic outpost for the U.S. Navy, providing support for military operations in the region. This military presence had a lasting impact on U.S.-Cuba relations, as it established the U.S. as a dominant force in the Caribbean.

The Guantanamo Naval Base continued to play a significant role during the Cold War, serving as a key outpost for U.S. intelligence gathering and counterterrorism efforts. The base's proximity to communist Cuba made it a crucial hub for monitoring Soviet activities in the region. This Cold War era significance further complicated the legal and political controversies surrounding the base.

Despite the controversies, the Guantanamo Naval Base has had a significant economic impact on the local Cuban community. The base has provided employment opportunities and economic stability for the surrounding area, contributing to the local economy.

However, the base's impact on human rights and international law has been a subject of intense debate. The detention facilities at Guantanamo have drawn international criticism for their treatment of detainees, raising questions about the base's adherence to human rights standards.

The future of the Guantanamo Naval Base remains uncertain, with potential implications for U.S.-Cuba relations. As diplomatic relations between the two countries continue to evolve, the future of the base will likely be a topic of negotiation and consideration.

In conclusion, the negotiations between the U.S. and Cuba for the establishment of the naval base in Guantanamo Bay have had far-reaching implications for U.S.-Cuba relations. From its early history to its role in intelligence gathering and counterterrorism efforts, the base has played a significant role in shaping the geopolitical landscape of the region. However, the base's impact on human rights, its economic significance, and its future remain topics of controversy and debate. Understanding the negotiations and their consequences is crucial for diplomats and historians studying the history of the U.S. Naval Base in Guantanamo Bay and its importance in U.S.-Cuba relations.

The construction and early operations of the base

The establishment and early history of the U.S. Naval Base in Guantanamo Bay, Cuba, holds great importance in understanding the dynamics of U.S.-Cuba relations. This section delves into the origins of the base, shedding light on its construction and early operations.

The U.S. Naval Base in Guantanamo Bay was established in 1903 as a result of the Cuban-American Treaty, which granted the United States control over this strategic piece of land. The construction of the base was a monumental task, involving the building of military installations, housing facilities, and support infrastructure. The United States invested significant resources in developing the base, transforming it into a key naval outpost in the Caribbean.

During the Spanish-American War in 1898, Guantanamo Bay played a pivotal role as a staging area for U.S. military operations. This conflict had a profound impact on U.S.-Cuba relations, as Cuba gained independence from Spain, and the United States emerged as a major power in the region. The establishment of the naval base further solidified American influence in Cuba and allowed for continued control over the island's affairs.

Throughout the Cold War, the Guantanamo Naval Base became even more significant in U.S.-Cuba relations. The base served as a crucial outpost for monitoring Soviet activities in the region and ensuring American national security. The tense relations between the United States and Cuba during this period further heightened the strategic importance of the base.

However, the Guantanamo Naval Base has not been without its share of legal and political controversies. Its presence on Cuban soil has long been a source of contention, with Cuba arguing that the lease agreement is invalid. The base has also been at the center of debates surrounding human rights and international law, particularly regarding the detention and treatment of prisoners at the Guantanamo Bay detention camp.

Apart from its military significance, the base has had a profound economic impact on the local Cuban community. The base has provided employment opportunities for Cubans and has contributed to the local economy through various economic activities.

As diplomatic and historical perspectives evolve, it becomes crucial to examine the future of the Guantanamo Naval Base and its potential impact on U.S.-Cuba relations. The changing dynamics in bilateral relations and the push for normalization of ties between the two countries raise questions about the future of the base and its role in promoting democracy and stability in Cuba.

In conclusion, understanding the construction and early operations of the U.S. Naval Base in Guantanamo Bay provides valuable insights into the history of U.S.-Cuba relations. The base's establishment, its role in historical conflicts, its legal and political controversies, its impact on the local community, and its future significance all contribute to a comprehensive understanding of this complex and controversial military installation.

The Role of the Guantanamo Naval Base in the Spanish-American War and its Impact on U.S.-Cuba Relations

The establishment and early history of the U.S. Naval Base in Guantanamo Bay, Cuba, holds significant importance in understanding the complex and evolving relationship between the United States and Cuba. This subchapter delves into the pivotal role played by the Guantanamo Naval Base during the Spanish-American War and its lasting impact on U.S.-Cuba relations.

During the late 19th century, tensions between the United States and Spain were escalating, with the latter holding control over Cuba. In 1898, the Spanish-American War erupted, and the Guantanamo Naval Base emerged as a strategic outpost for the U.S. Navy. Its geographical location, offering a deep-water harbor and proximity to the Caribbean and Latin America, made it an ideal location for the U.S. military.

The Guantanamo Naval Base played a crucial role in the war, serving as a vital supply and logistics hub for the U.S. Navy. It provided a safe haven for American ships and troops, enabling them to launch successful military operations against Spanish forces in Cuba. The U.S. victory in the war ultimately led to the end of Spanish rule in Cuba and marked the beginning of a new era in U.S.-Cuba relations.

The impact of the Spanish-American War on U.S.-Cuba relations cannot be overstated. With the defeat of Spain, the United States assumed temporary control over Cuba and established itself as a dominant power in the region. The Guantanamo Naval Base became a symbol of American influence and control over Cuban affairs, laying the foundation for future tensions between the two nations.

This subchapter explores the lasting impact of the Guantanamo Naval Base on U.S.-Cuba relations, examining how its establishment during the Spanish-American War set the stage for the complex dynamics that followed. It sheds light on the power dynamics between the United States and Cuba, with the naval base representing American military might and influence.

By examining the role of the Guantanamo Naval Base in the Spanish-American War and its subsequent impact on U.S.-Cuba relations, diplomats and historians gain valuable insights into the historical context that shaped the relationship between these two nations. This understanding provides a foundation for comprehending the legal, political, and economic controversies that have surrounded the Guantanamo Naval Base throughout its history and its potential implications for the future of U.S.-Cuba relations.

The significance of Guantanamo Bay during the Spanish-American War

During the late 19th century, the Spanish-American War marked a turning point in the relationship between the United States and Cuba. The conflict, which emerged out of Cuba's struggle for independence from Spain, had a profound impact on the establishment and importance of the U.S. Naval Base in Guantanamo Bay, Cuba.

As the war unfolded, the United States sought to secure its interests in the region and establish a strategic military presence in the Caribbean. In this context, Guantanamo Bay emerged as a crucial location due to its deep-water harbor and its proximity to both the United States and Cuba. Recognizing its potential, the U.S. Navy established a coaling station in Guantanamo Bay in 1898 and later expanded it into a full-fledged naval base.

The Guantanamo Naval Base played a pivotal role in the Spanish-American War. Its strategic location allowed the U.S. Navy to project its power and control the surrounding waters, facilitating the blockade of Spanish ships and the protection of American forces. The base also served as a crucial supply and logistical hub for American troops deployed in Cuba. Moreover, Guantanamo Bay provided a safe haven for American ships, protecting them from hostile encounters and offering a secure base for operations.

The establishment of the Guantanamo Naval Base significantly influenced U.S.-Cuba relations. By securing control over the base, the United States cemented its presence in Cuba and asserted its dominance in the region. The base became a symbol of American power projection and effectively served as a reminder of U.S. influence over Cuban affairs.

The significance of Guantanamo Bay during the Spanish-American War cannot be understated. It not only provided the U.S. Navy with a strategic advantage but also played a crucial role in shaping U.S.-Cuba relations. Today, the legacy of Guantanamo Bay continues to be a subject of debate and controversy, reflecting its lasting impact on both diplomatic and historical narratives.

The aftermath of the war and its impact on U.S.-Cuba relations

The end of any war brings forth a myriad of consequences that shape the future relationship between former adversaries. The aftermath of the Spanish-American War proved to be no exception, particularly in regards to U.S.-Cuba relations. This subchapter aims to delve into the repercussions of the war and how they influenced the dynamic between the two nations.

The Spanish-American War of 1898 marked a turning point in history for both the United States and Cuba. With the defeat of the Spanish forces, the United States emerged as a global power and gained control over territories including the Philippines, Puerto Rico, and Guam. In the case of Cuba, the U.S. military established a naval base in Guantanamo Bay, a move that would have far-reaching implications.

The establishment of the U.S. Naval Base in Guantanamo Bay signaled the beginning of a complex and often contentious relationship between the United States and Cuba. The base served as a strategic location for the U.S. military, providing a gateway to the Caribbean and allowing for greater control over the region. However, this presence also sparked concerns and grievances on the Cuban side, as it was seen as an infringement on their sovereignty.

Throughout the Cold War, the Guantanamo Naval Base played a significant role in U.S.-Cuba relations. The base became a symbol of the ideological divide between the United States and Cuba, with tensions escalating during the Cuban Missile Crisis in 1962. The presence of the base heightened the animosity between the two nations, further solidifying the divide.

The legal and political controversies surrounding the U.S. Naval Base in Guantanamo Bay further exacerbated the strained relations between the United States and Cuba. The base became a focal point for debates on human rights and international law, particularly regarding the treatment of detainees and the legal status of the base itself. These controversies only served to deepen the divide and hinder any potential progress in U.S.-Cuba relations.

Despite the numerous challenges and controversies, the Guantanamo Naval Base has played a vital role in U.S. efforts to promote democracy and stability in Cuba. The base has served as a platform for intelligence gathering and counterterrorism efforts, aiding U.S. endeavors to combat threats in the region. Additionally, the base has played a role in refugee processing and migration control, offering assistance to those seeking a better life.

As U.S.-Cuba relations continue to evolve, the future of the Guantanamo Naval Base remains uncertain. The potential impact of the base on the relationship between the two nations cannot be understated. Its closure or continued presence will undoubtedly shape the course of U.S.-Cuba relations, as both sides navigate the complexities of history, politics, and sovereignty.

In conclusion, the aftermath of the war and the establishment of the Guantanamo Naval Base had a profound impact on U.S.-Cuba relations. From the tensions of the Cold War to the legal controversies surrounding the base, its presence has shaped the dynamic between the two nations. As the future of the base remains uncertain, its potential impact on U.S.-Cuba relations continues to be a topic of great interest to diplomats and historians alike.

The role of the naval base in maintaining U.S. presence in the region

The Guantanamo Naval Base has played a crucial role in maintaining U.S. presence in the region throughout its history. Situated strategically in Guantanamo Bay, Cuba, the naval base has served as a vital outpost for the United States, enabling it to project its power and protect its interests in the Caribbean.

Since its establishment in 1903, the Guantanamo Naval Base has been integral to U.S.-Cuba relations. It has served as a symbol of American military might and a key platform for conducting various operations and exercises. During the early years, the base facilitated communication and support for U.S. naval forces operating in the Caribbean and Latin America.

The base's significance became even more pronounced during the Spanish-American War. Guantanamo Bay played a pivotal role as a coaling station and a safe harbor for the U.S. Navy. It allowed the U.S. to establish a naval blockade against Spanish forces and ultimately contributed to the U.S. victory in the war. This event solidified the strategic importance of the naval base and further shaped U.S.-Cuba relations.

Throughout the Cold War, the Guantanamo Naval Base took on a new role as a strategic outpost in the U.S. containment policy against the Soviet Union. The base provided a forward operating location for surveillance, intelligence gathering, and counterintelligence efforts. It served as a critical listening post, monitoring Soviet activities in the region and ensuring the U.S. had valuable information on potential threats.

Besides its military significance, the base has also been at the center of legal and political controversies. The detention facilities at Guantanamo Bay have raised concerns over human rights and international law. The treatment of detainees and the legal framework surrounding their detention have sparked widespread debate and criticism.

Despite these controversies, the Guantanamo Naval Base has been instrumental in U.S. efforts to promote democracy and stability in Cuba. It has facilitated refugee processing and migration control, helping manage the influx of Cuban migrants seeking asylum in the United States. The base has provided a safe haven for those fleeing political persecution and has contributed to U.S. humanitarian efforts in the region.

Looking ahead, the future of the Guantanamo Naval Base remains uncertain. The evolving U.S.-Cuba relations and changing geopolitical dynamics may impact its role and significance. However, the naval base's strategic location, historical importance, and multifaceted contributions ensure that it will continue to be a key factor in U.S. presence and engagement in the region. Diplomats and historians will undoubtedly continue to explore the complexities surrounding the base and its potential impact on U.S.-Cuba relations.

The Guantanamo Naval Base during the Cold War and its Significance in U.S.-Cuba Relations

The Guantanamo Naval Base, located in Guantanamo Bay, Cuba, played a significant role during the Cold War and continues to be a focal point in U.S.-Cuba relations. This subchapter delves into the historical context and explores the importance of the base in shaping diplomatic and historical narratives.

During the early years of the Cold War, the Guantanamo Naval Base served as a strategic location for the United States. Established in 1903 under the Platt Amendment, it provided the U.S. with a foothold in the Caribbean region, ensuring access to vital trade routes and serving as a strong military presence near potential threats. The base became even more crucial during the Cuban Revolution in 1959 when Fidel Castro came to power. As relations between the U.S. and Cuba deteriorated, Guantanamo remained a symbol of American influence and a strategic military outpost.

The base's significance in U.S.-Cuba relations is multifaceted. Firstly, it served as a staging ground for various military operations during the Cold War, including intelligence gathering and counterterrorism efforts. The Guantanamo Naval Base became an important hub for monitoring Soviet activities in the region, ensuring the U.S. had an upper hand in the global power struggle.

Secondly, the base played a role in refugee processing and migration control. As political and economic instability plagued Cuba, thousands of Cubans sought refuge in the U.S. The Guantanamo Naval Base became a temporary home for many refugees, highlighting the complexities of migration policies and the intersection of human rights and international law.

Moreover, the base became a subject of legal and political controversies, particularly concerning allegations of human rights abuses and the indefinite detention of individuals. These controversies continue to shape the narrative surrounding the base and its impact on U.S.-Cuba relations.

The Guantanamo Naval Base also had a significant economic impact on the local Cuban community. The base provided job opportunities and contributed to the local economy, creating a complex dynamic between the U.S. military presence and the Cuban population.

Looking towards the future, the subchapter explores the potential impact of the Guantanamo Naval Base on U.S.-Cuba relations. As both countries seek to normalize their diplomatic ties, the future of the base remains uncertain. Its closure or transformation could have far-reaching consequences for the relationship between the two nations.

In conclusion, the Guantanamo Naval Base holds immense historical and diplomatic significance in U.S.-Cuba relations. From its establishment during the Cold War to its role in intelligence gathering, migration control, and human rights controversies, the base has shaped the narrative of this complex relationship. Understanding the nuances of the base's history is crucial for diplomats and historians alike to comprehend the broader context of U.S.-Cuba relations and its implications for the future.

The naval base as a strategic outpost during the Cold War

The naval base in Guantanamo Bay, Cuba played a crucial role as a strategic outpost during the Cold War. As diplomats and historians examine the history of the U.S. Naval Base in Guantanamo, it becomes evident that its importance in U.S.-Cuba relations cannot be overstated.

During the early years of the Cold War, the Guantanamo Naval Base served as a critical location for monitoring and gathering intelligence on Soviet activities in the Caribbean region. Its proximity to the Soviet

Union's ally, Cuba, made it an ideal site for surveillance and reconnaissance missions. The base's strategic location allowed the United States to track Soviet naval movements, gather intelligence on their military capabilities, and maintain a strong presence in the region to deter potential threats.

In addition to its intelligence-gathering role, the Guantanamo Naval Base also served as a forward operating base for the U.S. Navy. It provided a secure harbor for American warships, submarines, and aircraft carriers, ensuring their readiness to respond to any potential Soviet aggression. The base's deep-water port and airfield facilities were instrumental in supporting U.S. military operations throughout the Cold War.

Moreover, the Guantanamo Naval Base also played a significant role in supporting U.S. efforts to promote democracy and stability in Cuba. It served as a symbol of American military power and commitment to the region, demonstrating to the Cuban government and the rest of Latin America that the United States would not tolerate the spread of communism. The presence of the base acted as a deterrent against any potential Cuban aggression, ensuring that the U.S. had a strong foothold in the region.

However, the Guantanamo Naval Base also faced its fair share of legal and political controversies. The lease agreement between the United States and Cuba, signed in 1903, has been a subject of contention. The Cuban government has repeatedly called for the base's closure, considering it a violation of their sovereignty. The base has also been the center of debates regarding human rights and international law, particularly with regards to the detention facilities established there.

As diplomats and historians explore the history and significance of the Guantanamo Naval Base, it becomes evident that its future will continue to impact U.S.-Cuba relations. The potential closure or repurposing of the base would have significant implications for both countries, affecting their political, economic, and security dynamics. Understanding the naval base's history is essential for comprehending the complex relationship between the United States and Cuba and the ongoing issues surrounding Guantanamo Bay.

The Cuban Missile Crisis and the tensions surrounding the base

The Cuban Missile Crisis of 1962 was a defining moment in the history of the U.S. Naval Base in Guantanamo Bay, Cuba. This subchapter examines the events leading up to the crisis and the subsequent tensions surrounding the base, providing insight into its significance in U.S.-Cuba relations.

During the Cold War, the Guantanamo Naval Base played a critical role in the United States' efforts to contain the spread of communism. However, tensions escalated dramatically when the Soviet Union, under the leadership of Nikita Khrushchev, decided to install nuclear missiles in Cuba, just 90 miles from U.S. soil. This move threatened the security of the United States and triggered a major international crisis.

The presence of the U.S. Naval Base in Guantanamo Bay became a focal point of the crisis. The base served as a strategic location for monitoring and gathering intelligence on Soviet activities in the region. As tensions escalated, the United States reinforced its military presence at the base, heightening the sense of unease between the two superpowers.

The Cuban Missile Crisis brought the world to the brink of nuclear war. Diplomats and historians recognize the pivotal role that the Guantanamo Naval Base played in this tense standoff. It served as a symbol of U.S. military might and a visible reminder of American influence on the island.

The crisis was ultimately resolved through a diplomatic agreement between President John F. Kennedy and Khrushchev, in which the

United States agreed to remove its missiles from Turkey in exchange for the removal of Soviet missiles from Cuba. However, tensions surrounding the base persisted, and its continued existence became a contentious issue in U.S.-Cuba relations.

Today, the Guantanamo Naval Base remains a source of controversy and a symbol of the complex relationship between the United States and Cuba. The base has been the subject of legal and political controversies, particularly regarding its use as a detention facility for suspected terrorists. The economic impact of the base on the local Cuban community has also been a topic of debate.

As diplomats and historians analyze the history of the U.S. Naval Base in Guantanamo Bay, it is crucial to understand the role it played during the Cuban Missile Crisis and the subsequent tensions that have shaped U.S.-Cuba relations. This subchapter provides a comprehensive examination of this pivotal period in history, shedding light on the significance of the base and its potential impact on future relations between the two nations.

The impact of the Cold War on U.S.-Cuba relations and the role of the naval base

The Cold War had a profound impact on U.S.-Cuba relations, and the Guantanamo Naval Base played a significant role in this dynamic. Throughout the Cold War, the United States and Cuba found themselves on opposing sides of the ideological divide, with Cuba aligning itself with the Soviet Union and the United States leading the Western bloc.

The Guantanamo Naval Base, established in 1903, became even more strategically important during the Cold War. As tensions between the United States and the Soviet Union escalated, the base served as a crucial outpost for intelligence gathering and surveillance. Its proximity to Cuba allowed the United States to monitor Soviet activities and gain valuable insights into their military capabilities. The presence of the base also acted as a deterrent, showcasing U.S. military power in the region.

The Cold War also witnessed several key events that further strained U.S.-Cuba relations and highlighted the significance of the naval base. One such event was the Bay of Pigs invasion in 1961, when U.S.-backed Cuban exiles attempted to overthrow Fidel Castro's regime. The naval base served as a staging ground for this ill-fated operation, which ultimately failed and deepened the animosity between the two nations.

Another pivotal moment was the Cuban Missile Crisis in 1962, when the world came perilously close to nuclear war. The discovery of Soviet missiles in Cuba prompted a tense standoff between the United States and the Soviet Union. The Guantanamo Naval Base played a crucial role during this crisis, serving as a base for U.S. forces and a potential target for Soviet retaliation. The crisis ultimately ended peacefully, but it further underscored the naval base's significance in U.S.-Cuba relations.

The Cold War also had legal and political implications for the Guantanamo Naval Base. The United States maintained control over the base through a lease agreement with Cuba, which became a source of controversy. As tensions between the two nations escalated, Cuba repeatedly called for the termination of the lease, arguing that it was an infringement on its sovereignty.

In conclusion, the Cold War had a transformative impact on U.S.-Cuba relations, and the Guantanamo Naval Base played a pivotal role in this complex dynamic. Serving as a strategic outpost, intelligence gathering hub, and staging ground for military operations, the base became a symbol of U.S. power and influence in the region. The legal and political controversies surrounding the base further complicated the relationship between the two nations. Understanding the historical context of the Cold War and the role of the naval base is essential for diplomats and historians to comprehensively analyze the intricacies of U.S.-Cuba relations.

Chapter 2: The Legal and Political Controversies Surrounding the U.S. Naval Base in Guantanamo Bay

The Legal Status of the Guantanamo Naval Base

The Guantanamo Naval Base, located in Guantanamo Bay, Cuba, has been a subject of legal and political controversy for many years. This subchapter explores the legal status of the base and its implications in the context of U.S.-Cuba relations.

The establishment of the U.S. Naval Base in Guantanamo Bay dates back to the early 20th century when the United States leased the land from Cuba under the 1903 Cuban-American Treaty. This lease agreement, known as the Guantanamo Bay Lease Agreement, granted the United States exclusive control and jurisdiction over the naval base, giving rise to its unique legal status.

Throughout its history, the Guantanamo Naval Base has played a significant role in U.S.-Cuba relations. During the Spanish-American War, the base served as a strategic outpost for the U.S. Navy, enabling them to project power in the Caribbean region. This military presence had a lasting impact on the relationship between the United States and Cuba, shaping their interactions during the Cold War.

The legal and political controversies surrounding the Guantanamo Naval Base have mainly revolved around issues of sovereignty and human rights. Critics argue that the base violates international law as it operates on Cuban territory without Cuba's consent. Moreover, the detention facilities at Guantanamo Bay, used to hold suspected terrorists, have drawn widespread condemnation for their treatment of prisoners and alleged human rights abuses.

The economic impact of the Guantanamo Naval Base on the local Cuban community is also a topic of interest. While the base provides employment opportunities for some Cubans, it has limited economic benefits due to its isolated nature and restrictions on interaction with the surrounding community.

Additionally, the base has played a significant role in intelligence gathering and counterterrorism efforts. Its strategic location and advanced facilities have made it an essential asset in U.S. national security operations, particularly in the fight against terrorism.

The future of the Guantanamo Naval Base holds potential implications for U.S.-Cuba relations. As diplomatic efforts between the two nations continue to evolve, questions arise regarding the base's longevity and its impact on future relations. Some argue that the closure of the Guantanamo Naval Base could serve as a symbolic gesture toward normalizing relations, while others emphasize its strategic importance in promoting democracy and stability in Cuba.

In conclusion, the legal status of the Guantanamo Naval Base has been a subject of ongoing debate, with implications for U.S.-Cuba relations, human rights, and international law. Understanding the complex history and controversies surrounding the base is essential for diplomats and historians interested in comprehending the broader context of U.S.-Cuba relations and the role of the Guantanamo Naval Base in shaping them.

The lease agreement between the U.S. and Cuba

The lease agreement between the U.S. and Cuba, signed in 1903, has been a central aspect of the history and controversy surrounding the Guantanamo Naval Base. This subchapter will delve into the intricacies of this agreement and shed light on its significance in U.S.-Cuba relations.

The lease agreement, also known as the Cuban-American Treaty, granted the United States the perpetual use and control of the Guantanamo Bay area, which spans approximately 45 square miles. In exchange, the U.S. pays an annual rent of $4,085, a sum that remains unchanged to this day. This agreement was initially negotiated as part of the Platt Amendment, a provision that allowed the U.S. to intervene in Cuban affairs.

The establishment of the U.S. Naval Base in Guantanamo Bay in 1903 was not without controversy. It occurred during a time of significant U.S. expansionism, and the base played a crucial role in projecting U.S. power in the Caribbean region. The lease agreement solidified the U.S. presence in Cuba and served as a strategic foothold for the United States throughout the 20th century.

During the Spanish-American War, the Guantanamo Naval Base played a pivotal role in the U.S. military's campaign against Spain. The base served both as a staging ground for military operations and as a vital supply depot. The war not only resulted in the liberation of Cuba from Spanish rule but also marked the beginning of a complicated relationship between the U.S. and Cuba, with the Guantanamo Naval Base at its core.

Throughout the Cold War, the Guantanamo Naval Base took on heightened significance. Its proximity to the Soviet Union made it an ideal location for monitoring Soviet activities and gathering intelligence. The base played a crucial role in the Cuban Missile Crisis, serving as a staging ground for U.S. military operations during the tense standoff between the U.S. and the Soviet Union.

The lease agreement has been a subject of legal and political controversies. Cuba has long argued that the lease is illegal and that the U.S. presence violates its sovereignty. This has led to ongoing debates and calls for the return of the base to Cuban control.

The Guantanamo Naval Base has also had a significant economic impact on the local Cuban community. The base has provided employment opportunities and generated revenue for the surrounding area. However, it has also created social and economic disparities, as the base operates under U.S. jurisdiction and is not subject to Cuban laws and regulations.

The base's role in intelligence gathering and counterterrorism efforts cannot be overstated. It has been used as a detention center for suspected terrorists, which has raised concerns about human rights and international law. The treatment of detainees and the legal framework surrounding their captivity have been highly controversial and have drawn international criticism.

The Guantanamo Naval Base has also been seen as a symbol of U.S. efforts to promote democracy and stability in Cuba. It has provided a platform for U.S. influence and has served as a refuge for Cuban refugees. The base has played a critical role in refugee processing and migration control, particularly during periods of political instability in Cuba.

Finally, the future of the Guantanamo Naval Base remains uncertain. Calls for its closure have grown louder in recent years, and its continued existence has the potential to impact U.S.-Cuba relations. The subchapter will explore the various perspectives on the base's future and its potential implications for the relationship between the two nations.

In conclusion, the lease agreement between the U.S. and Cuba has been a focal point of the history and controversies surrounding the Guantanamo Naval Base. Its establishment, impact on U.S.-Cuba relations, and significance in various areas such as intelligence gathering, human rights, and democracy promotion make it a crucial topic for diplomats and historians alike to understand.

The debate over the legality of the U.S. presence in Guantanamo Bay

As diplomats and historians delve into the rich history of the U.S. Naval Base in Guantanamo Bay, Cuba, one topic that continues to spark intense debate is the legality of the U.S. presence in this controversial territory. This subchapter aims to provide a comprehensive overview of the legal and political controversies surrounding the Guantanamo Naval Base, shedding light on the complex issues at play.

From its establishment in 1903, the U.S. Naval Base in Guantanamo Bay has been a focal point of U.S.-Cuba relations. Initially established as a coaling station during the Spanish-American War, the base quickly evolved into a strategic military outpost during the Cold War. However, its presence has been fraught with legal and political challenges.

Critics argue that the U.S. presence in Guantanamo Bay violates international law, citing the 1903 lease agreement between the U.S. and Cuba as a violation of Cuba's sovereignty. They contend that the indefinite detention of prisoners at the Guantanamo Bay detention camp, established in the early 2000s, is a clear violation of human rights and due process.

Proponents of the U.S. presence in Guantanamo Bay argue that the lease agreement grants the U.S. the right to maintain a naval base in the region, thereby justifying its continued presence. They maintain that the detention camp serves as a necessary tool in the fight against terrorism, allowing for the interrogation and treatment of individuals captured in the global war on terror.

The legal and political controversies surrounding Guantanamo Bay have had far-reaching consequences. The base has become a lightning rod for criticism from the international community, with many countries calling for its closure. The impact on U.S.-Cuba relations cannot be understated, as the Guantanamo Naval Base has been a constant source of tension between the two nations.

Furthermore, the economic impact of the base on the local Cuban community is a topic of concern. While the base provides employment opportunities, there are also concerns about the displacement of local residents and the environmental impact of the U.S. presence.

In conclusion, the debate over the legality of the U.S. presence in Guantanamo Bay is a complex and multifaceted issue. It encompasses questions of international law, human rights, and the broader political dynamics between the U.S. and Cuba. Understanding the various perspectives and controversies surrounding this topic is crucial for diplomats and historians seeking a comprehensive understanding of the Guantanamo Naval Base and its impact on U.S.-Cuba relations.

The implications of the legal status on U.S.-Cuba relations

The legal status of the U.S. Naval Base in Guantanamo Bay, Cuba has had significant implications on the relationship between the United States and Cuba throughout history. This subchapter explores the various ways in which the legal status of the base has shaped the dynamics between the two countries, from its establishment to the present day.

The establishment and early history of the U.S. Naval Base in Guantanamo Bay, Cuba, marked a turning point in U.S.-Cuba relations. The lease agreement signed in 1903 granted the United States control over the base in perpetuity, creating a unique legal entity separate from Cuban sovereignty. This arrangement has played a crucial role in shaping the power dynamics between the two countries, as it has allowed the United States to maintain a military presence just 90 miles off the coast of Cuba.

During the Spanish-American War, the Guantanamo Naval Base played a pivotal role in the U.S. military's efforts to gain control over Cuba. Its strategic location and deep-water harbor made it an ideal base for naval operations, and its establishment had a lasting impact on U.S.-Cuba relations. The base became a symbol of U.S. dominance in the region and served as a reminder of Cuba's status as a semi-sovereign nation. ·

Throughout the Cold War, the Guantanamo Naval Base took on added significance in U.S.-Cuba relations. As tensions between the United States and Cuba escalated, the base became a focal point for geopolitical rivalries. It served as a staging ground for U.S. military operations and intelligence gathering efforts, heightening the animosity between the two nations.

The legal and political controversies surrounding the Guantanamo Naval Base have further complicated U.S.-Cuba relations. The indefinite detention of prisoners at the Guantanamo Bay detention camp has been a subject of international criticism and has strained diplomatic ties between the United States and Cuba. The legal status of the base has also been a source of contention, with Cuba calling for the return of the territory and the United States asserting its rights under the lease agreement.

The economic impact of the Guantanamo Naval Base on the local Cuban community cannot be understated. While the base has provided employment opportunities for some Cubans, it has also created a sense of dependency on the United States. The base's presence has influenced the local economy and has shaped the socio-economic dynamics of the surrounding region.

In conclusion, the legal status of the U.S. Naval Base in Guantanamo Bay has had far-reaching implications on U.S.-Cuba relations. It has played a significant role in shaping the power dynamics between the two countries, from its establishment to the present day. The base's strategic importance, legal controversies, economic impact, and role in intelligence gathering have all contributed to the complex relationship between the United States and Cuba. As the future of the Guantanamo Naval Base remains uncertain, its potential impact on U.S.-Cuba relations continues to be a topic of great interest and debate among diplomats and historians alike.

The Political Controversies Surrounding the Guantanamo Naval Base

The Guantanamo Naval Base, located in Cuba, has been at the center of numerous political controversies throughout its history. As diplomats and historians, it is crucial to understand these controversies in order to gain a comprehensive understanding of the base's significance in U.S.-Cuba relations.

One of the earliest controversies surrounding the Guantanamo Naval Base emerged during its establishment and early history. The United States secured a lease for the base in 1903, granting them control over the area while recognizing Cuban sovereignty. This arrangement has been a subject of contention, with some arguing that the lease infringes upon Cuban sovereignty and is a relic of imperialistic policies.

The Spanish-American War also contributed to political controversies surrounding the Guantanamo Naval Base. Following the war, the United States maintained a military presence in Cuba, including at Guantanamo. This presence exacerbated tensions between the two nations and played a significant role in shaping U.S.-Cuba relations during the early 20th century.

During the Cold War, the Guantanamo Naval Base gained further significance in U.S.-Cuba relations. It became a strategic location for the United States to monitor Soviet activities in the region. However, this heightened military presence sparked protests and anti-American sentiments, leading to increased political controversies both domestically and internationally.

The legal and political controversies surrounding the Guantanamo Naval Base reached a peak in the 21st century. Following the September 11 attacks, the United States used the base as a detention center for suspected terrorists. The indefinite detention, interrogation techniques, and lack of due process for detainees sparked widespread condemnation from the international community, human rights organizations, and even some American politicians.

These controversies also raised questions about the base's impact on human rights and international law. The treatment of detainees and the legal justifications for their detention raised concerns about the United States' adherence to international legal standards and human rights principles.

Furthermore, the Guantanamo Naval Base's future has become a topic of debate in recent years. As the United States seeks to normalize relations with Cuba, there have been calls to close the base or renegotiate the lease agreement. The potential impact of such a decision on U.S.-Cuba relations remains uncertain.

In conclusion, the Guantanamo Naval Base has been embroiled in numerous political controversies throughout its history. From questions of sovereignty to concerns about human rights and international law, these controversies have shaped U.S.-Cuba relations and continue to be of great importance to diplomats and historians. Understanding these controversies is crucial in order to gain a comprehensive understanding of the base's significance and its potential impact on the future of U.S.-Cuba relations.

The opposition to the U.S. presence in Guantanamo Bay by the Cuban government

The opposition to the U.S. presence in Guantanamo Bay by the Cuban government has been a central issue in the history of the U.S.-Cuba relations. Since its establishment in 1903, the U.S. Naval Base in Guantanamo Bay has been a point of contention between the two countries.

The Cuban government has consistently voiced its opposition to the presence of the U.S. in Guantanamo Bay, considering it a violation of their sovereignty. They argue that the lease agreement, which grants the U.S. perpetual control over the base, is unfair and should be terminated. The Cuban government has repeatedly called for the return of the territory to Cuban sovereignty, seeing the U.S. presence as a relic of imperialism.

The opposition to the U.S. presence in Guantanamo Bay is deeply rooted in the historical context of U.S.-Cuba relations. The base played a significant role in the Spanish-American War, where the U.S. military used it as a strategic outpost to control the region. This history has fueled the Cuban government's resentment towards the U.S. presence, as they see it as a symbol of past aggression.

Furthermore, the Cuban government has raised concerns about the legal and political controversies surrounding the base. The detention facility established in Guantanamo Bay, where suspected terrorists are held without trial, has been a source of international criticism. The Cuban government has condemned the violation of human rights and international law associated with this facility, further fueling their opposition to the U.S. presence.

Additionally, the economic impact of the base on the local Cuban community has been a source of contention. While the base provides employment opportunities for some Cubans, others argue that it limits their access to resources and restricts economic development in the region.

Overall, the opposition to the U.S. presence in Guantanamo Bay by the Cuban government is a complex issue deeply intertwined with the history and politics of U.S.-Cuba relations. It raises questions about sovereignty, human rights, and international law. As diplomats and historians, it is crucial to understand and analyze this opposition to gain a comprehensive understanding of the dynamics at play in the U.S.-Cuba relationship. The future of the Guantanamo Naval Base remains uncertain, and its potential impact on U.S.-Cuba relations will continue to be a subject of debate and negotiation.

The domestic and international political debates surrounding the base

As diplomats and historians, it is essential to delve into the domestic and international political debates surrounding the Guantanamo Naval Base. Throughout its history, the base has been at the center of numerous controversies and has played a pivotal role in shaping U.S.-Cuba relations.

One of the key areas of debate is the legal and political controversies surrounding the base. The United States continues to lease the land from Cuba under a perpetual lease agreement signed in 1903. However, Cuba considers the lease agreement to be invalid and has consistently called for the base's closure. This ongoing dispute has fueled tensions between the two nations and has been a topic of international concern.

Furthermore, the Guantanamo Naval Base has been a subject of intense scrutiny in terms of human rights and international law. The detention facility established at the base following the 9/11 attacks has been the center of controversy. The treatment of detainees and the use of enhanced interrogation techniques have raised questions about human rights violations and adherence to international legal standards.

Additionally, the base's role in intelligence gathering and counterterrorism efforts has sparked debates on both domestic and international fronts. The U.S. government has argued that the base is crucial for gathering intelligence and detaining individuals deemed threats to national security. However, critics argue that the base's operations infringe upon civil liberties and undermine the rule of law.

Another significant point of contention is the economic impact of the Guantanamo Naval Base on the local Cuban community. The base has provided employment opportunities and economic stability for the surrounding area. However, the Cuban government has criticized the base, arguing that it represents a neocolonial presence on their soil.

Looking ahead, the future of the Guantanamo Naval Base remains uncertain and continues to raise political debates. The Obama administration made efforts to close the detention facility, citing human rights concerns, but faced significant domestic opposition. With the changing political landscape, it is crucial to explore the potential impact the base's closure or continued operation may have on U.S.-Cuba relations.

In conclusion, the domestic and international political debates surrounding the Guantanamo Naval Base have been multifaceted and complex. From legal and political controversies to economic impact and human rights concerns, the base's history and future continue to shape U.S.-Cuba relations. As diplomats and historians, it is vital to understand and analyze these debates to gain a comprehensive understanding of the base's significance.

The impact of the controversies on U.S. foreign policy and diplomatic relations

The impact of the controversies surrounding the Guantanamo Naval Base on U.S. foreign policy and diplomatic relations has been significant and far-reaching. This subchapter examines the various legal and political issues that have arisen in relation to the base and their implications for the United States' interactions with Cuba and the wider international community.

One of the key controversies surrounding the Guantanamo Naval Base is its establishment and continued presence on Cuban soil. The base was established in 1903 as a result of the Platt Amendment, which granted the United States the right to intervene in Cuban affairs. This arrangement has been a constant source of tension in U.S.-Cuba relations, with Cuba repeatedly calling for the base's closure and the return of the territory to Cuban control.

The Guantanamo Naval Base played a significant role in the Spanish-American War, further complicating its relationship with Cuba. The base served as a strategic location for the U.S. Navy during the war and its aftermath, leading to increased American influence in Cuba. This has had a lasting impact on U.S.-Cuba relations, with the base representing a symbol of American imperialism in the eyes of many Cubans.

During the Cold War, the Guantanamo Naval Base became even more significant in U.S.-Cuba relations. It served as a key base for intelligence gathering and counterterrorism efforts, particularly during the Cuban Missile Crisis. The base's proximity to Cuba made it an ideal location for monitoring Soviet activities in the region. However, this heightened military presence further strained diplomatic relations between the two countries.

The legal and political controversies surrounding the Guantanamo Naval Base have also had a profound impact on U.S. foreign policy. The base has been the subject of numerous legal challenges, particularly in relation to the detention of suspected terrorists following the 9/ 11 attacks. The United States' use of the base as a detention center for enemy combatants has drawn international criticism and raised concerns about human rights and international law.

The economic impact of the Guantanamo Naval Base on the local Cuban community cannot be overlooked. The base has provided employment opportunities for many Cubans, particularly in the form of jobs supporting the base's operations. However, this economic reliance on the base has also made the local community vulnerable to changes in U.S. policy, leading to uncertainty and economic instability.

Looking to the future, the fate of the Guantanamo Naval Base remains uncertain. Its potential impact on U.S.-Cuba relations is still a subject of debate. Some argue that the base should be closed as a gesture of goodwill towards Cuba and to improve diplomatic relations, while others believe it should be maintained to protect U.S. interests in the region.

In conclusion, the controversies surrounding the Guantanamo Naval Base have had a profound impact on U.S. foreign policy and diplomatic relations. From the base's establishment and role in historical conflicts to the legal and political controversies of recent years, its significance cannot be understated. As diplomats and historians, it is crucial to understand and analyze these controversies to gain a comprehensive understanding of the complex U.S.-Cuba relationship and its wider implications for international relations.

Chapter 3: The Economic Impact of the Guantanamo Naval Base on the Local Cuban Community

The Economic Benefits of the Naval Base for the Cuban Community

The Guantanamo Naval Base, located in Guantanamo Bay, Cuba, has played a significant role in the economic development of the local Cuban community. Over the years, the base has provided numerous economic opportunities and has contributed to the growth and stability of the region.

One of the primary ways in which the naval base benefits the Cuban community is through job creation. The base employs a large number of local residents, offering them stable and well-paying jobs. These jobs range from administrative and support staff to skilled laborers and contractors. The base's presence has helped to reduce unemployment rates in the area and has provided a source of income for many Cuban families.

In addition to direct employment, the naval base has also stimulated economic growth through indirect means. The base requires various goods and services to operate effectively, and local businesses have been able to capitalize on this demand. Restaurants, hotels, transportation services, and other businesses have thrived as a result of the base's presence. This has led to increased tourism and investment in the region, providing further economic opportunities for the Cuban community.

Furthermore, the naval base has contributed to the development of infrastructure in Guantanamo Bay. The base requires access to reliable utilities, such as electricity, water, and telecommunications. Consequently, the Cuban government has invested in improving the infrastructure in the surrounding areas to meet the base's needs. This has resulted in improved living conditions for the local population, with better access to essential services and amenities.

The economic benefits of the naval base extend beyond Guantanamo Bay. The base has provided opportunities for trade and commerce between the United States and Cuba. The flow of goods and services between the two countries has created a mutually beneficial economic relationship, stimulating growth in both economies.

In conclusion, the Guantanamo Naval Base has had a positive impact on the local Cuban community in terms of job creation, economic growth, and infrastructure development. The base has provided employment opportunities, stimulated local businesses, and fostered trade between the United States and Cuba. As the future of the naval base remains uncertain, it is crucial to consider these economic benefits when evaluating its importance in U.S.-Cuba relations.

The creation of jobs and economic opportunities

The creation of jobs and economic opportunities at the Guantanamo Naval Base has played a significant role in the history of U.S.-Cuba relations. This subchapter explores how the base has contributed to the local Cuban community and the broader economic impact it has had.

From its establishment in 1903, the Guantanamo Naval Base has been a source of employment for the local population. The base has created jobs in various sectors, including construction, maintenance, and support services. The presence of the base has provided a stable source of income for many Cubans, boosting the local economy and providing opportunities for economic advancement.

During the early years of the base, its construction and development created a surge in economic activity. The influx of American personnel and investment stimulated the local economy, leading to the growth of businesses and infrastructure in the surrounding areas. The base became a hub of economic activity, attracting workers and entrepreneurs who sought to take advantage of the opportunities it presented.

Furthermore, the Guantanamo Naval Base has played a vital role in trade between the United States and Cuba. As a strategic location for maritime transportation, the base has facilitated the movement of goods and resources, contributing to the economic development of both countries. The base has served as a significant trading point, fostering economic ties and encouraging economic cooperation between the two nations.

However, the economic impact of the base has not been without controversy. The base's presence has been a subject of political debate and has faced opposition from some Cubans who view it as a symbol of American imperialism. The economic benefits derived from the base have not always been evenly distributed, leading to economic disparities within the local community.

Despite these controversies, the Guantanamo Naval Base continues to provide economic opportunities for the Cuban population. The base remains an important source of employment, offering jobs and economic stability to many individuals and families. Its presence has helped sustain local businesses and industries, contributing to the overall economic well-being of the region.

In conclusion, the creation of jobs and economic opportunities at the Guantanamo Naval Base has had a significant impact on U.S.-Cuba relations. The base has been a source of employment, fostering economic development and trade between the two countries. While controversies surround its existence, the base's economic contributions cannot be overlooked. As diplomats and historians delve into the history of the U.S. Naval Base in Guantanamo Bay, they must recognize the complex interplay between economics, politics, and international relations that have shaped its role in the broader context of U.S.-Cuba relations.

The support provided to local businesses and infrastructure

The support provided to local businesses and infrastructure in the Guantanamo Naval Base is an important aspect to consider when examining the overall impact of the base on the local Cuban community. Throughout its history, the base has provided various forms of support that have contributed to the development and sustainability of the local economy and infrastructure.

One of the key ways in which the base has supported local businesses is through employment opportunities. The base employs a significant number of local residents, providing them with stable jobs and income. This has not only helped to alleviate unemployment in the region but has also created opportunities for skill development and career advancement. The base has also facilitated business partnerships and contracts with local suppliers, thereby stimulating economic activity and supporting the growth of local enterprises.

In addition to employment, the base has also played a role in supporting infrastructure development in the surrounding area. The presence of the base has necessitated the establishment of transportation networks, communication systems, and utilities, which have not only benefited the base itself but have also had spill-over effects on the local community. The development of roads, bridges, and other infrastructure has improved connectivity and accessibility, making it easier for local businesses to transport goods and services.

Furthermore, the base has contributed to the provision of essential services such as healthcare and education. The base has established medical facilities that not only serve the military personnel but also provide medical assistance to local residents. Similarly, educational institutions have been established to cater to the educational needs of military personnel and their families, but they have also opened their doors to local students.

However, it is important to acknowledge that the support provided by the base is not without controversy. Critics argue that the economic benefits have not been distributed equitably, with some local businesses benefiting more than others. Additionally, there are concerns about the environmental impact of the base on the surrounding area.

Understanding the support provided to local businesses and infrastructure in the Guantanamo Naval Base is crucial to comprehending the complex dynamics of the base's relationship with the local community. It is essential to recognize both the positive contributions and the challenges associated with this support, as it shapes the overall impact of the base on U.S.-Cuba relations and the local economy. By examining these aspects, diplomats and historians can gain a comprehensive understanding of the multifaceted nature of the Guantanamo Naval Base and its significance in the broader context of U.S.-Cuba relations.

The contribution to the overall economy of the region

The Guantanamo Naval Base in Cuba has played a significant role in the overall economy of the region throughout its history. From its establishment during the Spanish-American War to its current status as a controversial detainment facility, the base has had a profound impact on the local Cuban community and the broader economy.

During the early years of the base's establishment, it served as a vital economic hub, providing employment opportunities for the local population. The construction and maintenance of the base required a significant workforce, leading to the creation of jobs in various sectors such as construction, transportation, and administration. These employment opportunities provided a source of income for many Cuban families, contributing to the overall economic growth of the region.

Furthermore, the base's presence also stimulated the growth of ancillary industries. Local businesses, such as restaurants, shops, and hotels, emerged to cater to the needs of the American personnel stationed at the base. These establishments not only provided goods and services to the military personnel but also created employment opportunities for the local population.

The Guantanamo Naval Base also had a positive impact on the region's trade and commerce. The base served as a strategic port for the United States, facilitating the transportation of goods and supplies between the United States and Cuba. This resulted in increased trade activities and boosted the local economy.

However, it is important to note that the economic impact of the base has not been without controversy. The base has been a subject of political and legal disputes, which have had implications for the local economy. The detainment facility at Guantanamo, particularly in recent years, has attracted international criticism and affected the reputation of the base. This has led to a decline in tourism and investment, which has had adverse effects on the local businesses that rely on these industries.

In conclusion, the Guantanamo Naval Base has played a significant role in the overall economy of the region. Its establishment and operations have provided employment opportunities, stimulated ancillary industries, and facilitated trade and commerce. However, the controversies surrounding the base, particularly the detainment facility, have had negative implications for the local economy. As the future of the base remains uncertain, it is crucial to consider the potential impact on the economic relationship between the United States and Cuba.

The Challenges and Disruptions Caused by the Naval Base

The Guantanamo Naval Base has been a source of controversy and disruption throughout its history, posing numerous challenges to both the United States and Cuba. This subchapter explores the various difficulties and disruptions that have arisen as a result of the naval base's existence, shedding light on its impact on U.S.-Cuba relations.

From its establishment in 1903, the Guantanamo Naval Base has been a constant source of tension between the two nations. Its presence has been seen by many as a violation of Cuba's sovereignty, leading to ongoing legal and political controversies surrounding its legitimacy. Diplomats and historians alike have grappled with the complex legal framework surrounding the base, which has resulted in disputes and strained relations between the two countries.

The economic impact of the naval base on the local Cuban community has been a significant challenge. While it has provided some employment opportunities for the local population, it has also disrupted traditional industries and hindered economic development. The base's self-sufficiency has created a separate economy, detached from the rest of Cuba, leading to inequality and resentment among the local population.

The naval base's role in intelligence gathering and counterterrorism efforts has also presented challenges. Its controversial detention facilities, most notably during the War on Terror, have raised concerns about human rights abuses and violated international law. The base's impact on human rights and international law has been a subject of intense scrutiny and criticism from the international community.

Furthermore, the Guantanamo Naval Base has played a role in U.S. efforts to promote democracy and stability in Cuba. Its presence has been seen by some as a symbol of American imperialism, undermining the United States' credibility in its democracy promotion efforts. The base's association with refugee processing and migration control has also contributed to its complicated legacy, with debates surrounding the treatment of refugees and the violation of their rights.

Looking towards the future, the naval base's potential impact on U.S.-Cuba relations remains uncertain. As diplomatic relations continue to evolve, the fate of the base hangs in the balance. The potential closure or continued operation of the Guantanamo Naval Base will undoubtedly have far-reaching implications for both countries, further shaping their complex relationship.

In conclusion, the Guantanamo Naval Base has posed numerous challenges and disruptions to both the United States and Cuba. From legal and political controversies to economic disparities and human rights concerns, the base's existence has had a profound impact on U.S.-Cuba relations. As diplomats and historians continue to study this complex issue, it is essential to understand the multifaceted challenges and disruptions caused by the naval base.

The limitations on the Cuban community's access to certain areas of Guantanamo Bay

The limitations on the Cuban community's access to certain areas of Guantanamo Bay have been a significant aspect of the U.S.-Cuba relations and have sparked a great deal of controversy over the years. This subchapter aims to shed light on the various factors that have contributed to these limitations and their implications.

One of the primary reasons behind the restrictions imposed on the Cuban community's access to certain areas of Guantanamo Bay is the

U.S. government's concern for national security. Given the strategic importance of the naval base, the U.S. has implemented strict measures to safeguard sensitive areas and classified information. As a result, access to these areas is heavily regulated, and only authorized personnel are granted entry. This has naturally limited the Cuban community's ability to freely explore and utilize these parts of the bay.

Another factor contributing to these limitations is the legal framework surrounding the Guantanamo Naval Base. The base is governed by a lease agreement between the U.S. and Cuba, known as the 1903 Cuban-American Treaty. According to this treaty, the U.S. has exclusive control and jurisdiction over the base, while Cuba retains sovereignty. This unique arrangement has created a complex legal environment, making it challenging for the Cuban community to assert their rights and access certain areas freely.

Furthermore, the political tensions between the U.S. and Cuba have played a significant role in restricting access to Guantanamo Bay. The long-standing animosity and strained diplomatic relations have influenced the U.S.'s decision-making regarding the base. The U.S. government has been cautious about allowing too much interaction between the Cuban community and the naval base, as it fears a potential security threat or espionage.

These limitations on access have had a considerable economic impact on the local Cuban community. The base, being a major employer in the region, has provided job opportunities and generated revenue for the surrounding area. However, the restrictions on access have prevented the Cuban community from fully benefiting from these economic opportunities, resulting in limited employment prospects and economic growth.

In conclusion, the limitations on the Cuban community's access to certain areas of Guantanamo Bay have been influenced by national security concerns, legal complexities, and political tensions. While these restrictions have undoubtedly played a role in safeguarding U.S. interests, they have also had implications for the local Cuban community, both economically and socially. Understanding these limitations is crucial in comprehending the dynamics of the U.S.-Cuba relations and the overall significance of the Guantanamo Naval Base.

The environmental impact of the base on the surrounding areas

The establishment and operation of the U.S. Naval Base in Guantanamo Bay, Cuba, has had significant environmental implications for the surrounding areas. This subchapter will explore the various ways in which the base has affected the natural environment and local ecosystems.

One of the key environmental concerns associated with the base is the impact on marine life. The base is located in a pristine coastal area, home to a diverse range of marine species. The construction and maintenance of the base have resulted in habitat destruction and pollution. The dredging of the bay for the construction of the base's infrastructure has disrupted the natural flow of water, affecting the marine ecosystem. The discharge of pollutants from naval activities, such as fuel spills and wastewater discharge, has further deteriorated the water quality, threatening the survival of marine species.

Additionally, the base has caused deforestation in the surrounding areas. The need for infrastructure and resources has led to the clearing of large areas of land, resulting in the loss of valuable habitats for native plants and animals. This deforestation has also contributed to soil erosion and increased the risk of landslides, further compromising the local ecosystem.

The base's activities have also had an impact on air quality. The naval operations, including aircraft flights and the use of heavy machinery, have contributed to air pollution through the release of greenhouse gases and other pollutants. This has not only affected the air quality within the base but has also had implications for the nearby communities.

Furthermore, the base's waste management practices have raised concerns about the disposal of hazardous materials. Improper handling and disposal of waste, including chemicals and other toxic substances, have the potential to contaminate the soil and groundwater, posing a threat to both human health and the environment.

Addressing these environmental concerns is crucial for the preservation of the surrounding ecosystems and the well-being of local communities. It requires close collaboration between the U.S. and Cuban authorities to develop and implement sustainable practices within the base. This includes improved waste management systems, the promotion of renewable energy sources, and the establishment of protected areas to conserve and restore the natural habitats that have been impacted by the base's presence.

In conclusion, the U.S. Naval Base in Guantanamo Bay has had a significant environmental impact on the surrounding areas. The destruction of marine habitats, deforestation, air and water pollution, and inadequate waste management practices have all contributed to the degradation of the natural environment. Recognizing these concerns and taking proactive measures to mitigate the environmental impact is essential for the sustainable coexistence of the base and the surrounding ecosystems.

The economic dependence and vulnerability of the local community

The economic dependence and vulnerability of the local community surrounding the Guantanamo Naval Base is a crucial aspect that must be discussed in the context of U.S.-Cuba relations. For decades, the base has had a profound impact on the economic well-being of the nearby Cuban community, creating both opportunities and challenges.

Since its establishment in 1903, the Guantanamo Naval Base has been a major source of employment for the local population. The base has provided jobs in various sectors, including construction, maintenance, administration, and support services. This economic activity has ensured a stable income for many families and has been the primary source of livelihood for the community.

However, the local community's economic dependence on the naval base has also made it vulnerable to fluctuations in U.S.-Cuba relations. During times of tension or political disputes between the two countries, there have been instances when the base has been partially or completely closed, leading to significant job losses and economic hardships for the local residents.

Moreover, the economic benefits derived from the naval base have not been evenly distributed among the local population. Many of the higher-paying jobs at the base have been occupied by U.S. citizens or individuals with strong connections to the U.S. military. This has created a sense of inequality and resentment among the local community, who feel that they have been relegated to lower-paying and less prestigious positions.

The economic impact of the naval base has also had broader implications for the Cuban economy as a whole. The base has provided a significant source of revenue for the Cuban government through lease payments and other financial agreements. However, this reliance on a foreign military presence has raised questions about Cuba's sovereignty and its ability to shape its own economic destiny.

In conclusion, the economic dependence and vulnerability of the local community surrounding the Guantanamo Naval Base is a complex issue that cannot be overlooked in discussions about U.S.-Cuba relations. While the base has provided employment opportunities for the local population, it has also created economic inequalities and made the community susceptible to political tensions between the two countries. It is essential for diplomats and historians to examine this aspect of the base's impact to gain a comprehensive understanding of its role in the broader context of U.S.-Cuba relations.

Chapter 4: The Role of the Guantanamo Naval Base in Intelligence Gathering and Counterterrorism Efforts

The Naval Base as a Hub for Intelligence Operations

Intelligence operations have been an integral part of the Guantanamo Naval Base's history, playing a crucial role in shaping U.S.-Cuba relations and global security efforts. This subchapter explores the significance of the base as a hub for intelligence gathering and counterterrorism efforts, shedding light on its impact on diplomacy, national security, and international law.

Since its establishment, the Guantanamo Naval Base has been strategically positioned to monitor and gather intelligence on activities in the Caribbean region. Its location provided the United States with a vantage point for surveillance and information collection during critical moments in history. During the Spanish-American War, the base played a vital role in tracking Spanish naval movements and providing intelligence support to U.S. forces. This early experience laid the groundwork for the base's future intelligence operations.

The Cold War era saw a significant expansion of intelligence activities at Guantanamo. The base became a key listening post, intercepting and analyzing communications from Soviet vessels and submarines in the region. These efforts played a pivotal role in monitoring Soviet military activities and contributed to U.S. national security during a tense period of global conflict.

In response to evolving security threats, the Guantanamo Naval Base became an essential hub for counterterrorism operations. Following the September 11, 2001 attacks, the base played a central role in intelligence gathering and detention of suspected terrorists. The detention facility, known as Guantanamo Bay Detention Camp, became a focal point of controversy, sparking debates about human rights, international law, and the treatment of detainees.

The intelligence gathered at Guantanamo has not only served U.S. interests but has also contributed to global security efforts. The base's strategic location and comprehensive surveillance capabilities have facilitated the monitoring of illicit activities, such as drug trafficking and human smuggling, in the region. This intelligence sharing with partner nations has strengthened regional security and enhanced cooperation against common threats.

However, the role of the Guantanamo Naval Base in intelligence operations has not been without controversy. The detention facility's practices have raised concerns about human rights abuses and the adherence to international law. Efforts to close the facility and address these legal and political controversies have been ongoing, sparking debates among diplomats, historians, and human rights advocates.

Looking towards the future, the Guantanamo Naval Base's potential impact on U.S.-Cuba relations remains uncertain. As diplomatic efforts between the two nations evolve, the base's role in intelligence gathering, counterterrorism, and refugee processing may undergo significant changes. The outcome of these developments will have implications not only for U.S.-Cuba relations but also for regional stability and global security efforts.

In conclusion, the Guantanamo Naval Base has served as a vital hub for intelligence operations throughout its history. From monitoring Spanish naval movements to intercepting Soviet communications, the base's strategic location has enabled the gathering of critical intelligence. However, controversies surrounding human rights, international law, and the detention facility have also overshadowed its contributions. As the future of the base and its impact on U.S.-Cuba relations remains uncertain, diplomats, historians, and policymakers must closely monitor and analyze the evolving dynamics to navigate the complexities of intelligence operations, diplomacy, and national security.

The role of Guantanamo Bay in gathering intelligence on regional and global threats

The Guantanamo Naval Base has long played a significant role in gathering intelligence on regional and global threats, serving as a vital hub for the United States in its efforts to maintain national security. This subchapter delves into the crucial role that Guantanamo Bay has played in intelligence gathering and counterterrorism efforts, highlighting its importance in safeguarding the interests of not only the United States but also its allies.

Since its establishment, Guantanamo Bay has operated as a strategic location for gathering intelligence on various regional and global threats. Its location in close proximity to Latin America and the Caribbean has allowed the United States to monitor and gather information on potential threats emanating from these regions. The base's advanced surveillance capabilities, coupled with its access to advanced technology and intelligence resources, have made it an invaluable asset in the fight against terrorism and other transnational threats.

Guantanamo Bay has served as a key intelligence gathering center, facilitating the collection of vital information on terrorist organizations, drug trafficking networks, and other criminal enterprises. The base has been instrumental in tracking and disrupting illicit activities, providing intelligence agencies with critical insights into the operations and intentions of these entities.

Furthermore, Guantanamo Bay has played a pivotal role in coordinating intelligence sharing efforts with international partners. Through its collaborative relationships with foreign intelligence agencies, the base has fostered vital information exchanges, strengthening global counterterrorism efforts and enhancing collective security.

However, it is important to acknowledge that Guantanamo Bay's intelligence gathering activities have not been without controversy. The base has faced significant criticism for its treatment of detainees and alleged human rights abuses. The subchapter will explore the legal and political controversies surrounding Guantanamo Bay, shedding light on the challenges and ethical dilemmas that arise in the pursuit of intelligence gathering.

In conclusion, Guantanamo Bay has emerged as a critical intelligence gathering center, enabling the United States to effectively monitor and combat regional and global threats. As diplomats and historians delve into the history of the U.S. Naval Base in Guantanamo Bay, it becomes evident that its role in intelligence gathering has been instrumental in shaping U.S.-Cuba relations, regional stability, and global security.

The collaboration between U.S. intelligence agencies and the naval base

The Guantanamo Naval Base has played a crucial role in intelligence gathering and counterterrorism efforts for the United States. Throughout its history, the collaboration between U.S. intelligence agencies and the naval base has been instrumental in ensuring national security and protecting American interests. This subchapter explores the significance of this collaboration and its impact on U.S.-Cuba relations.

From its establishment in 1903, the Guantanamo Naval Base has served as a strategic location for U.S. intelligence operations. Its proximity to Cuba and other Latin American countries has allowed for effective monitoring of regional activities. Over the years, the base has hosted various intelligence agencies, including the Central Intelligence Agency (CIA) and the National Security Agency (NSA), who have utilized its facilities to conduct surveillance, intercept communications, and gather crucial information.

During the Cold War, the Guantanamo Naval Base became even more critical in U.S. intelligence efforts. Its location provided a vantage point for monitoring Soviet activities in Cuba and the surrounding region. The base played a pivotal role in detecting and intercepting Soviet submarines, ensuring the United States maintained a strong defense posture. This collaboration between U.S. intelligence agencies and the naval base significantly contributed to the containment of Soviet influence in the Western Hemisphere and safeguarded American national security interests.

In the post-9/11 era, the Guantanamo Naval Base has become synonymous with the detention and interrogation of suspected terrorists. U.S. intelligence agencies have been actively involved in gathering intelligence from detainees held at the base. However, the methods employed and the legal and political controversies surrounding these practices have raised concerns about human rights and international law.

Despite the controversies, the collaboration between U.S. intelligence agencies and the naval base has been vital in preventing terrorist attacks and ensuring the safety of American citizens. The base's strategic location and advanced surveillance capabilities have allowed for effective monitoring of terrorist activities in the region, acting as a deterrent to potential threats.

Looking ahead, the future of the Guantanamo Naval Base remains uncertain. As U.S.-Cuba relations continue to evolve, the base's role in intelligence gathering and counterterrorism efforts may change. However, its historical significance and the expertise developed through collaboration with U.S. intelligence agencies cannot be understated. The lessons learned and the knowledge gained from this collaboration will continue to shape U.S. efforts to promote democracy, stability, and national security in Cuba and the wider region. Diplomats and historians will continue to analyze the impact of this collaboration on U.S.-Cuba relations and its influence on global security dynamics.

In conclusion, the collaboration between U.S. intelligence agencies and the Guantanamo Naval Base has been crucial in gathering intelligence, countering threats, and protecting American interests. The naval base's strategic location and advanced capabilities have contributed significantly to U.S. national security efforts. However, it is essential to navigate the legal and political controversies surrounding the base's operations to ensure the protection of human rights and adherence to international law. As the future of the Guantanamo Naval Base unfolds, its potential impact on U.S.-Cuba relations and the global security landscape remains an area of great interest for diplomats and historians alike.

The impact of the intelligence activities on U.S. national security

The impact of intelligence activities on U.S. national security is a crucial aspect of the Guantanamo Naval Base's history and its importance in U.S.-Cuba relations. Diplomats and historians have long studied the intricate relationship between intelligence gathering, counterterrorism efforts, and national security. This subchapter aims to shed light on how the intelligence activities at the Guantanamo Naval Base have influenced U.S. national security over the years.

Since its establishment, the Guantanamo Naval Base has played a pivotal role in intelligence gathering. Situated strategically in close proximity to Cuba, it has served as a valuable outpost for monitoring activities in the region. Through the deployment of advanced surveillance technology and skilled personnel, the base has provided the U.S. with vital intelligence on various threats to national security, including those originating from Cuba.

During the Cold War era, the Guantanamo Naval Base became even more significant. It served as a key surveillance point for monitoring Soviet activities in the region, including missile installations in Cuba. The intelligence gathered from the base played a crucial role in ensuring U.S. national security during this tense period of superpower rivalry.

In recent years, the Guantanamo Naval Base has been involved in counterterrorism efforts. With its unique location and advanced facilities, the base has been utilized for detaining and interrogating individuals suspected of involvement in terrorist activities. While this aspect has been subject to controversy and legal challenges, the intelligence gathered through these efforts has undoubtedly contributed to U.S. national security by thwarting potential threats and disrupting terrorist networks.

However, the intelligence activities at the Guantanamo Naval Base have also raised concerns regarding human rights and international law. The treatment of detainees and the legality of their detention have been hotly debated topics. Critics argue that these activities have undermined the U.S.'s reputation and its commitment to upholding human rights and international legal standards.

As the future of the Guantanamo Naval Base remains uncertain, its potential impact on U.S.-Cuba relations cannot be ignored. The base has been a longstanding point of contention between the two countries, and any decisions regarding its fate will undoubtedly have consequences for the bilateral relationship.

In conclusion, the intelligence activities at the Guantanamo Naval Base have had a significant impact on U.S. national security. While providing valuable intelligence and contributing to counterterrorism efforts, these activities have also raised legal and ethical concerns. Understanding the complexities and implications of the intelligence activities at the base is essential for diplomats and historians analyzing the history and importance of the Guantanamo Naval Base in U.S.-Cuba relations.

The Counterterrorism Efforts and Detention Facilities at Guantanamo Bay

The Guantanamo Naval Base, located on the southeastern coast of Cuba, has been at the center of numerous legal and political controversies since its establishment. While it has played a significant role in U.S.-Cuba relations throughout history, one aspect that has garnered international attention is its role in counterterrorism efforts and detention facilities.

Following the September 11, 2001 terrorist attacks, the United States launched a global war on terror. As part of these efforts, the Guantanamo Naval Base became a crucial hub for detaining and interrogating individuals suspected of terrorism. The base's detention facilities, known as Guantanamo Bay detention camp or Gitmo, were designed to hold individuals captured during military operations in Afghanistan and other parts of the world.

The detention facilities at Guantanamo Bay became a subject of intense scrutiny due to allegations of human rights abuses, including torture and indefinite detention without trial. Critics argue that the treatment of detainees violates international law and tarnishes the United States' reputation as a defender of human rights.

Despite the controversies, U.S. officials maintain that the Guantanamo Naval Base and its detention facilities serve a critical purpose in the fight against terrorism. They argue that detaining suspected terrorists at Guantanamo Bay allows for effective intelligence gathering and prevents dangerous individuals from returning to the battlefield.

Over the years, efforts have been made to address the legal and political challenges surrounding Guantanamo Bay. Various court cases have challenged the legality of the detention facilities and the treatment of detainees. Additionally, some detainees have been transferred to other countries or released as part of efforts to close the detention camp.

The future of the Guantanamo Naval Base and its detention facilities remains uncertain. The Obama administration made attempts to close the detention camp, but faced significant obstacles in doing so. The Trump administration, on the other hand, expressed support for keeping the facility open and even considering sending new detainees there.

As diplomats and historians, it is essential to examine the counterterrorism efforts and detention facilities at Guantanamo Bay within the larger context of U.S.-Cuba relations, human rights, and international law. The Guantanamo Naval Base raises important questions about the balance between national security and individual rights, the impact of U.S. actions on its global image, and the evolving nature of counterterrorism efforts in the 21st century.

The establishment and operation of the detention facilities

The establishment and operation of the detention facilities at the Guantanamo Naval Base have been a topic of intense debate and controversy. This subchapter aims to provide a comprehensive understanding of the historical background, legal implications, and political considerations surrounding these facilities.

The detention facilities at Guantanamo Bay were established in 2002, following the September 11th terrorist attacks. The United States government designated the base as a location for detaining individuals captured in its global war on terror. These facilities were specifically designed to hold "enemy combatants" who were deemed a threat to national security.

The operation of the detention facilities has been subject to numerous legal and political controversies. One of the primary concerns raised by human rights organizations and international bodies is the indefinite detention of individuals without charge or trial. Critics argue that this violates basic principles of due process and the right to a fair trial.

The legal status of the detainees has also been a matter of contention. The U.S. government has argued that they are not entitled to the same legal protections as prisoners of war under the Geneva Conventions. Instead, they are considered "unlawful enemy combatants" and subject to military jurisdiction.

The conditions within the detention facilities have also come under scrutiny. Reports of torture, abuse, and inhumane treatment have raised serious concerns about human rights violations. These allegations have further fueled the controversy surrounding the Guantanamo Naval Base.

The operation of the detention facilities has had a significant impact on U.S.-Cuba relations. The Cuban government has long demanded the return of the base to Cuban sovereignty, viewing it as a violation of their territorial integrity. The presence of the detention facilities has further strained this already fragile relationship.

Furthermore, the economic impact of the Guantanamo Naval Base on the local Cuban community cannot be overlooked. While the base has provided employment opportunities for some, it has also led to heightened tensions and resentment among the local population.

Looking ahead, the future of the Guantanamo Naval Base remains uncertain. Calls for its closure have been persistent, with critics arguing that it serves as a recruitment tool for extremists and tarnishes the United States' reputation as a champion of human rights. However, the base continues to serve as a vital component of U.S. intelligence gathering and counterterrorism efforts.

In conclusion, the establishment and operation of the detention facilities at the Guantanamo Naval Base have been the subject of intense scrutiny and controversy. The legal, political, and human rights implications surrounding these facilities have had a profound impact on U.S.-Cuba relations. The future of the base and its potential impact on these relations remain uncertain, as the debate continues to unfold.

The controversies surrounding the treatment of detainees

The controversies surrounding the treatment of detainees at the Guantanamo Naval Base have been a subject of intense debate and scrutiny in recent years. This subchapter aims to shed light on the legal and political issues that have surrounded the treatment of detainees at this highly controversial facility.

One of the most significant controversies surrounding the treatment of detainees at Guantanamo is the use of enhanced interrogation techniques, commonly referred to as torture. The United States has faced widespread condemnation from international human rights organizations and legal experts for its use of techniques such as waterboarding, sensory deprivation, and stress positions. Critics argue that these techniques violate the United Nations Convention Against Torture and Other Cruel, Inhuman or Degrading Treatment or Punishment, to which the U.S. is a signatory.

Another controversy is the indefinite detention of individuals without charge or trial. Many detainees have been held at Guantanamo for years without being formally charged with any crime. This has raised serious concerns about due process and the right to a fair trial. Critics argue that this violates international human rights standards and undermines the principles of justice and the rule of law.

Furthermore, the treatment of detainees at Guantanamo has also raised questions about the United States' compliance with international law. The Guantanamo Naval Base is located on Cuban territory, yet the U.S. argues that it is not subject to Cuban jurisdiction or the protections of the Cuban legal system. This has led to a legal and political dispute between the U.S. and Cuba, with the Cuban government demanding the return of the base and condemning the treatment of detainees.

The controversies surrounding the treatment of detainees at Guantanamo have also had a significant impact on U.S.-Cuba relations. The existence of the base and the treatment of detainees have been a major source of tension between the two countries. Cuba has repeatedly called for the closure of the base, viewing it as a symbol of U.S. imperialism and a violation of its sovereignty.

In conclusion, the treatment of detainees at the Guantanamo Naval Base has been a highly controversial issue, raising concerns about torture, due process, and international law. These controversies have not only had an impact on U.S. foreign relations, particularly with Cuba, but also on the broader issues of human rights and the rule of law. It is crucial for diplomats and historians to examine these controversies in order to gain a comprehensive understanding of the complex legal and political issues surrounding the Guantanamo Naval Base.

The effectiveness of the counterterrorism efforts conducted at the naval base

One of the crucial aspects of the Guantanamo Naval Base is its role in intelligence gathering and counterterrorism efforts. The base has been an essential asset in the United States' fight against terrorism, particularly in the aftermath of the September 11, 2001 attacks.

The counterterrorism efforts conducted at the naval base have been highly effective in preventing future acts of terrorism and safeguarding national security. Through its intelligence capabilities and strategic location, the base has played a pivotal role in gathering crucial information on terrorist organizations and their activities. The naval base's proximity to the Caribbean and South America has allowed for enhanced monitoring of drug trafficking routes, which are often used by terrorist networks to finance their operations.

Moreover, the Guantanamo Naval Base has served as a vital center for conducting interrogations of high-value detainees, providing valuable intelligence on terrorist networks and their plans. The base's facilities, such as the detention center, have been specifically designed to house and interrogate individuals deemed a threat to national security. Although controversial, the interrogations have yielded valuable intelligence that has helped disrupt terrorist plots and save lives.

The effectiveness of the counterterrorism efforts at the base is further highlighted by the fact that no major terrorist attack has been successfully orchestrated from Guantanamo Bay. This achievement is a testament to the dedication and professionalism of the military personnel and intelligence agencies operating at the base.

However, it is important to note that the counterterrorism efforts at the naval base have faced criticism and legal challenges. The detention center has been a subject of controversy due to allegations of human rights abuses and the indefinite detention of individuals without trial. These issues have sparked debates surrounding the base's compliance with international law and human rights standards.

Nonetheless, it is undeniable that the counterterrorism efforts conducted at the Guantanamo Naval Base have been instrumental in protecting national security and preventing further acts of terrorism. The base's intelligence capabilities, strategic location, and specialized facilities have contributed significantly to the United States' ongoing fight against global terrorism.

In conclusion, the naval base's effectiveness in counterterrorism efforts has been a vital component of its overall importance in U.S.-Cuba relations. While controversies surrounding human rights and legal issues persist, it is crucial to recognize the significant contributions of the base in safeguarding national security and combating terrorism. The continued success of these efforts will undoubtedly shape the future of the Guantanamo Naval Base and its impact on U.S.-Cuba relations.

Chapter 5: The Impact of the Guantanamo Naval Base on Human Rights and International Law

The Violations of Human Rights at Guantanamo Bay

In this subchapter, we delve into the deeply troubling issue of human rights violations that have occurred at the Guantanamo Bay detention center. This topic is of utmost importance to diplomats and historians, as it sheds light on the complexities of the U.S.-Cuba relations and the legal and political controversies surrounding the Guantanamo Naval Base.

Since its establishment, Guantanamo Bay has become synonymous with human rights abuses and violations of international law. The treatment of detainees at the detention center has raised serious concerns about the U.S. commitment to upholding human rights and the rule of law.

One of the most contentious issues surrounding Guantanamo Bay is the indefinite detention of individuals without trial or due process. Many detainees have been held for years without being charged with any crime, violating their fundamental right to a fair trial. This blatant disregard for the principles of justice has drawn widespread condemnation from the international community.

Furthermore, reports of torture and mistreatment of detainees have surfaced, tarnishing the reputation of the United States as a champion of human rights. The use of enhanced interrogation techniques, such as waterboarding, has been widely criticized as not only inhumane but also ineffective in gathering reliable intelligence.

The existence of secret prisons, known as "black sites," within the Guantanamo Bay facility has also raised serious concerns. These covert operations undermine the principles of transparency and accountability, making it difficult to determine the extent of human rights abuses that have occurred.

The establishment of Guantanamo Bay as a detention center for suspected terrorists has had far-reaching implications for human rights and international law. The indefinite detention, torture, and lack of due process have eroded the principles on which the modern legal system is based.

The violations of human rights at Guantanamo Bay have not only had a detrimental impact on the detainees themselves but also on the reputation and credibility of the United States. Diplomats and historians must critically examine these violations to understand the broader implications for U.S.-Cuba relations and the fight for democracy and stability in Cuba.

As we explore the future of the Guantanamo Naval Base, it is crucial to address these human rights concerns and work towards rectifying the injustices that have occurred. Only by acknowledging and rectifying these violations can the United States regain its moral authority and promote a more just and humane world.

The allegations of torture and mistreatment of detainees

The allegations of torture and mistreatment of detainees at the Guantanamo Naval Base have been a source of controversy and international criticism since its establishment. This subchapter delves into the deeply troubling aspects of the base's history, raising important questions about human rights and international law.

The allegations of torture and mistreatment stem primarily from the post-9/11 era when the United States launched its "War on Terror."

In response to the attacks, the Guantanamo Naval Base became a key site for detaining individuals suspected of terrorism. The base's remote location and legal ambiguity allowed for the creation of a detention center where detainees were held without trial or due process.

Numerous reports and testimonies have emerged, providing evidence of torture and mistreatment at Guantanamo. Detainees have alleged being subjected to various forms of abuse, including physical and psychological torture, sexual humiliation, and prolonged solitary confinement. These allegations have raised serious concerns among human rights organizations, diplomats, and historians, who argue that such practices violate international law and undermine fundamental human rights.

The mistreatment of detainees at Guantanamo has also strained the United States' relations with other countries. Diplomatic tensions have arisen as allegations of torture and abuse have been made public, leading to calls for the closure of the detention center. The international community has condemned the practices at Guantanamo, viewing them as a violation of the Geneva Conventions and other international treaties.

Furthermore, the mistreatment of detainees has had a profound impact on the reputation of the United States as a champion of human rights and democracy. Critics argue that the use of torture and indefinite detention undermines the values and principles upon which the nation was founded. These allegations have also fueled anti-American sentiment and provided propaganda material for extremist groups.

Efforts to address the allegations of torture and mistreatment at Guantanamo have been met with significant legal and political challenges. Despite numerous calls for accountability and closure, the detention center remains operational, and detainees continue to languish without trial or release. The legal and political controversies surrounding the base have become a stain on the United States' human rights record, undermining its credibility on the global stage.

In conclusion, the allegations of torture and mistreatment of detainees at the Guantanamo Naval Base have had far-reaching implications on U.S.-Cuba relations, human rights, and international law. The controversy surrounding the base highlights the need for a thorough examination of the practices and policies that have allowed such abuses to occur. It is crucial for diplomats and historians to explore the ramifications of these allegations and advocate for justice, accountability, and respect for human rights in any discussions surrounding the future of the Guantanamo Naval Base.

The legal challenges and debates surrounding the treatment of detainees

The legal challenges and debates surrounding the treatment of detainees at the Guantanamo Naval Base have been a topic of immense controversy and scrutiny. This subchapter delves into the complex legal and political issues that have arisen in relation to the treatment of detainees, shedding light on the implications for human rights and international law.

Since its establishment, the Guantanamo Naval Base has been used as a detention facility for individuals believed to be involved in acts of terrorism or posing a threat to national security. However, the treatment of these detainees has been subject to intense criticism, raising concerns about their legal rights and the adherence to international law.

One of the primary legal challenges surrounds the indefinite detention of individuals without trial or charge. Critics argue that this violates the fundamental principle of habeas corpus, which guarantees the right to a fair trial and challenges the legality of prolonged detention without due process. Consequently, this has sparked numerous legal battles and debates over the extent of the U.S. government's authority in holding detainees at Guantanamo.

Another contentious issue is the use of enhanced interrogation techniques, including waterboarding and other forms of torture. These practices have been widely condemned by human rights organizations and scholars, who argue that they violate the prohibition of torture under international law. The legal status of these techniques and the responsibility of the U.S. government in employing them have been subjects of intense debate and litigation.

Furthermore, the question of jurisdiction and the applicability of domestic and international law at Guantanamo has been a significant legal challenge. The base is situated on Cuban territory but operated by the United States, creating a legal gray area. Determining which legal framework applies and how to ensure accountability for any violations has been a source of ongoing debate.

These legal challenges and debates have far-reaching implications not only for the treatment of detainees at Guantanamo but also for broader questions of human rights, international law, and the United States' commitment to upholding legal standards. Diplomats and historians will find this subchapter essential in understanding the legal complexities surrounding the treatment of detainees at the Guantanamo Naval Base and its impact on U.S.-Cuba relations, as well as broader global discussions on human rights and counterterrorism efforts.

The implications for international human rights standards

The establishment and continued operation of the Guantanamo Naval Base in Cuba have raised significant concerns regarding international human rights standards. This subchapter delves into the profound implications that the base has on human rights and international law, providing diplomats and historians with a comprehensive understanding of this complex issue.

One of the key concerns is the treatment of detainees held at Guantanamo Bay. The base gained notoriety for its role in the War on Terror, particularly for the detention and interrogation of suspected terrorists. The use of enhanced interrogation techniques, such as waterboarding, has been widely criticized as a violation of international human rights law, including the United Nations Convention Against Torture.

Furthermore, the indefinite detention of individuals without charge or trial also raises serious human rights concerns. Many detainees have been held at Guantanamo for years, without access to legal representation or the opportunity to challenge their detention. This practice contradicts fundamental principles of due process and the right to a fair trial, enshrined in international human rights instruments.

The use of military commissions at Guantanamo has also been subject to criticism. These special courts, established to try detainees, have been perceived as lacking the necessary independence and impartiality to ensure a fair trial. This raises concerns about the right to a fair and public hearing, as well as the right to an effective remedy.

The international community has consistently called for the closure of the Guantanamo Naval Base, citing its negative impact on human rights standards. The continued operation of the base undermines the credibility of the United States as a promoter and defender of human rights worldwide.

Addressing these human rights concerns is crucial for the United States to regain its standing as a global leader in the protection of human rights. It requires a comprehensive reassessment of the legal and political controversies surrounding Guantanamo Bay, as well as a commitment to upholding international human rights standards.

In conclusion, the implications for international human rights standards stemming from the Guantanamo Naval Base are significant and demand attention. By examining the treatment of detainees, the use of military commissions, and the practice of indefinite detention, diplomats and historians can gain a deeper understanding of the base's impact on human rights and international law. This knowledge is essential for shaping future policies and decisions related to Guantanamo and its potential impact on U.S.-Cuba relations.

The Legality of Detentions and Military Commissions at Guantanamo Bay

The issue of detentions and military commissions at Guantanamo Bay has been a subject of legal and political controversy for years. This subchapter explores the legality of these practices and their implications for international law and human rights.

Since its establishment, the Guantanamo Naval Base has been used as a detention facility for individuals captured during the U.S. war on terror. These detainees, often labeled as "enemy combatants," have been held without trial or access to legal representation, raising concerns about their rights and the legality of their detention.

One of the main legal justifications for the detentions has been the Authorization for Use of Military Force (AUMF) passed by the U.S. Congress in the aftermath of the September 11 attacks. This legislation granted the President broad powers to detain individuals associated with Al-Qaeda and the Taliban. However, critics argue that the AUMF does not provide a legal basis for indefinite detention or for the establishment of military commissions.

The establishment of military commissions at Guantanamo Bay has also faced legal challenges. These commissions, intended to try detainees for war crimes, have been criticized for their lack of transparency and adherence to due process. The Supreme Court has ruled that certain aspects of the military commissions violated constitutional and international law, leading to reforms and revisions.

The international community has also raised concerns about the legality of detentions and military commissions at Guantanamo. Many argue that these practices violate the Geneva Conventions and other international treaties on human rights. The indefinite detention without charge or trial, as well as the use of enhanced interrogation techniques, have been widely condemned as violating basic principles of human rights and the rule of law.

The legal and political controversies surrounding Guantanamo Bay have had a significant impact on U.S.-Cuba relations. The detention facility has been a source of tension between the two countries, with Cuba calling for the base's closure and the return of the territory to Cuban sovereignty. The international criticism of Guantanamo has also tarnished the United States' reputation and raised concerns about its commitment to human rights and the rule of law.

The future of detentions and military commissions at Guantanamo Bay remains uncertain. While some detainees have been transferred or released, others continue to be held without trial. The closing of the detention facility and the resolution of legal issues surrounding Guantanamo are complex and politically sensitive matters that will require careful consideration and cooperation between the United States and Cuba.

In conclusion, the legality of detentions and military commissions at Guantanamo Bay has been a subject of intense legal and political debate. The practices have raised concerns about human rights and the rule of law, both domestically and internationally. The resolution of these controversies and the future of Guantanamo will have significant implications for U.S.-Cuba relations and the promotion of democracy and stability in the region.

The legal framework governing the detentions and military commissions

The legal framework governing the detentions and military commissions at the Guantanamo Naval Base has been a subject of intense controversy and debate. This subchapter aims to provide diplomats and historians with an overview of the legal and political issues surrounding this aspect of the base.

Since its establishment, the Guantanamo Naval Base has been used to detain individuals suspected of terrorism and to conduct military commissions for those accused of committing war crimes. The legal framework governing these detentions and commissions is complex and has evolved over time.

Initially, the detentions at Guantanamo were carried out under the authority of the 2001 Authorization for Use of Military Force (AUMF), which granted the President broad powers to detain individuals associated with Al-Qaeda or the Taliban. However, the lack of a clear legal framework and the indefinite nature of the detentions raised concerns about due process and human rights.

In response to these concerns, the Supreme Court ruled in 2004, in the landmark case of Rasul v. Bush, that the detainees at Guantanamo had the right to challenge their detention in U.S. courts through habeas corpus petitions. This decision led to a series of legal battles and the development of new legal procedures for the detainees.

In 2006, the Military Commissions Act (MCA) was enacted to establish a legal framework for the military commissions at

Guantanamo. These commissions were intended to try individuals for war crimes and other offenses, but they were heavily criticized for their lack of procedural safeguards and their departure from traditional legal standards.

Subsequent legal challenges and changes in the law, including the Supreme Court's decision in Hamdan v. Rumsfeld in 2006, led to further modifications of the legal framework for the detentions and military commissions at Guantanamo. These changes aimed to address some of the due process concerns and to bring the procedures more in line with international legal standards.

Despite these efforts, the detentions and military commissions at Guantanamo continue to be the subject of legal and political controversies. Critics argue that the legal framework is still inadequate and that the detainees should either be released or transferred to the United States for trial in civilian courts.

In conclusion, the legal framework governing the detentions and military commissions at the Guantanamo Naval Base has been the source of significant legal and political controversies. The evolving nature of this framework reflects the ongoing struggle to balance security concerns with the protection of human rights and the rule of law.

The international criticism and legal challenges to the processes

The international criticism and legal challenges to the processes at the Guantanamo Naval Base have been significant and continue to shape the discussions surrounding its existence. Diplomats and historians have closely followed the controversies and legal battles that have emerged over the years. This subchapter aims to provide an overview of these criticisms and challenges, shedding light on the complex nature of the base's operations.

One of the primary concerns raised by the international community is the issue of human rights and international law. Critics argue that the detention center at Guantanamo Bay has violated fundamental principles of due process and the prohibition of torture. The indefinite detention of individuals without charge or trial has been a particularly contentious issue, leading to accusations of human rights abuses and undermining the credibility of the United States as a champion of human rights.

Moreover, the use of military commissions to try detainees instead of civilian courts has been a subject of intense legal debate. Critics argue that these commissions lack the necessary independence and transparency to ensure fair trials, thereby violating the principles of justice and the right to a fair trial.

The treatment of detainees, including reports of torture and abuse, has sparked international condemnation and legal challenges. The infamous images of detainees subjected to inhumane treatment have tarnished the reputation of the United States and fueled criticism from human rights organizations and foreign governments.

The lack of clarity regarding the legal status of detainees has also been a contentious issue. The classification of detainees as "enemy combatants" rather than prisoners of war has allowed for their indefinite detention without the protections afforded by the Geneva Conventions. This has been a focal point of legal challenges, with critics arguing that the United States is sidestepping its international obligations.

In addition to human rights concerns, the existence of the Guantanamo Naval Base has strained diplomatic relations between the United States and other countries. Many nations have called for the closure of the base, viewing it as a symbol of American imperialism and a violation of Cuban sovereignty. The base has been a recurring point of contention in U.S.-Cuba relations, hindering efforts to normalize diplomatic ties between the two countries.

In conclusion, the international criticism and legal challenges to the processes at the Guantanamo Naval Base have been substantial. Concerns over human rights, due process, and the base's impact on diplomatic relations have fueled ongoing debates and legal battles. As diplomats and historians examine the history and significance of the base, it is crucial to consider these criticisms and challenges to gain a comprehensive understanding of its complex legacy.

The impact on U.S. credibility and commitment to the rule of law

The Guantanamo Naval Base has long been a subject of controversy, particularly with regards to its impact on U.S. credibility and commitment to the rule of law. This subchapter delves into the legal and political issues surrounding the base, shedding light on its implications for U.S. foreign policy and international relations.

One of the key concerns regarding Guantanamo is the erosion of U.S. credibility in upholding the rule of law. The indefinite detention of individuals without trial and the use of enhanced interrogation techniques have raised serious questions about the United States' commitment to human rights and international law. Diplomats and historians must grapple with the implications of these practices on the country's image as a champion of justice and due process.

Moreover, the legal controversies surrounding the Guantanamo Naval Base have strained U.S. relations with the international community. The base's existence outside the jurisdiction of U.S. courts and the application of military commissions have been seen by many as a circumvention of legal norms. This has led to criticism from foreign governments, human rights organizations, and even some U.S. allies, who argue that such practices undermine the credibility of the U.S. legal system and its commitment to international law.

The impact on U.S.-Cuba relations is another aspect to consider. The continued presence of the Guantanamo Naval Base has been a constant source of tension between the two countries. Cuba views the base as a symbol of U.S. imperialism and a violation of its sovereignty. For diplomats and historians, it is crucial to examine the historical context and the role of the base in shaping U.S.-Cuba relations over the years, from the Spanish-American War to the Cold War and beyond.

Furthermore, the Guantanamo Naval Base has played a significant role in intelligence gathering and counterterrorism efforts. Its location in close proximity to Latin America and the Caribbean has made it a strategic asset for monitoring regional security threats. However, the methods employed in this pursuit have raised concerns about the balance between national security and human rights.

In conclusion, the impact of the Guantanamo Naval Base on U.S. credibility and commitment to the rule of law cannot be overlooked. Diplomats and historians must analyze the legal and political controversies surrounding the base, its economic impact on the local Cuban community, its role in intelligence gathering and counterterrorism, and its implications for human rights and international law. Understanding these issues is crucial in assessing the significance of the base in U.S. efforts to promote democracy, stability, and its future impact on U.S.-Cuba relations.

Chapter 6: The Significance of the Guantanamo Naval Base in U.S. Efforts to Promote Democracy and Stability in Cuba

The Naval Base as a Symbol of U.S. Support for Democracy in Cuba

Throughout its history, the U.S. Naval Base in Guantanamo Bay has served as a powerful symbol of American support for democracy in Cuba. This subchapter will explore the significance of the base in U.S.-Cuba relations, highlighting its role in promoting stability, human rights, and democratic values.

From its establishment in 1903, the Guantanamo Naval Base has played a crucial role in shaping the relationship between the United States and Cuba. Initially established as a coaling station, it quickly evolved into a strategic outpost during the Spanish-American War. The base's presence allowed the U.S. to project its power in the region and exert influence over Cuba's political affairs.

During the Cold War, the Guantanamo Naval Base took on added importance. As tensions between the U.S. and Cuba escalated, the base became a critical hub for intelligence gathering and counterterrorism efforts. Its strategic location enabled the U.S. to monitor Soviet activity in the region and protect American interests.

However, the Guantanamo Naval Base has not been without controversy. Its legal and political controversies have sparked international debate and raised questions about its compliance with human rights and international law. The detention center established at the base following the September 11 attacks became particularly contentious, with allegations of human rights abuses and violations of due process.

Despite these controversies, the Guantanamo Naval Base has also had a positive impact on the local Cuban community. The base has provided employment opportunities and economic stability, benefiting the surrounding area. Additionally, the base has played a crucial role in processing refugees and controlling migration, ensuring the safety and well-being of those seeking asylum.

Looking ahead, the future of the Guantanamo Naval Base remains uncertain. As diplomatic relations between the U.S. and Cuba continue to evolve, there are ongoing discussions about the base's future. However, its potential impact on U.S.-Cuba relations should not be underestimated. The base has historically been a symbol of American commitment to democracy and stability in Cuba, and any change in its status will undoubtedly have far-reaching consequences.

In conclusion, the U.S. Naval Base in Guantanamo Bay has been a significant symbol of American support for democracy in Cuba. Its establishment and early history, its role in the Spanish-American War and the Cold War, and its impact on human rights, international law, and economic development have all shaped its importance in U.S.-Cuba relations. As the future of the base remains uncertain, its potential impact on diplomatic efforts and the promotion of democratic values cannot be overlooked.

The role of Guantanamo Bay in U.S. efforts to promote democracy in Cuba

Throughout its history, the Guantanamo Naval Base has played a significant role in U.S. efforts to promote democracy and stability in Cuba. This subchapter will delve into the various ways in which

Guantanamo Bay has been utilized as a tool for advancing these objectives.

One of the key aspects to consider is the base's establishment and early history. From its inception, the U.S. Naval Base in Guantanamo Bay has served as a symbol of American presence and influence in the region. This presence has been instrumental in projecting democratic values and principles throughout Cuba, despite the challenges posed by the Cuban government.

During the Spanish-American War, the Guantanamo Naval Base played a crucial role in U.S.-Cuba relations. The base served as a strategic location for U.S. military operations and allowed for the projection of American power in the region. This presence not only helped secure Cuba's independence but also laid the foundation for future efforts to promote democracy on the island.

Throughout the Cold War, Guantanamo Bay continued to be of immense significance in U.S.-Cuba relations. The base became a focal point for intelligence gathering, monitoring the activities of the Soviet Union, and countering potential threats to regional stability. By maintaining a presence in Guantanamo, the United States demonstrated its commitment to supporting democratic ideals and protecting the interests of the Cuban people.

However, the Guantanamo Naval Base has not been without its controversies. The legal and political issues surrounding the base have been the subject of intense scrutiny. The detention center established at Guantanamo has been a source of concern, with debates surrounding human rights and international law. Despite these controversies, the United States has remained committed to promoting democracy and stability in Cuba.

The economic impact of the Guantanamo Naval Base on the local Cuban community cannot be overlooked. The base has provided employment opportunities and economic stability for many individuals in the region. This has helped to foster a sense of stability and progress, further promoting democratic values in Cuba.

Looking ahead, the future of the Guantanamo Naval Base will undoubtedly impact U.S.-Cuba relations. As diplomatic efforts continue, it is crucial to assess the potential impact of any changes to the base on the promotion of democracy and stability in Cuba.

In conclusion, the Guantanamo Naval Base has played a multifaceted role in U.S. efforts to promote democracy in Cuba. From its establishment and early history to its involvement in intelligence gathering, counterterrorism efforts, and refugee processing, the base has been vital in projecting democratic values and stability on the island. Despite the controversies surrounding the base, its economic impact on the local community and its potential future implications cannot be overlooked. Understanding the significance of the Guantanamo Naval Base is essential for diplomats and historians studying the history of U.S.-Cuba relations and the promotion of democracy in Cuba.

The support provided to Cuban dissidents and opposition groups

Throughout its history, the U.S. Naval Base in Guantanamo Bay has played a critical role in supporting Cuban dissidents and opposition groups. This subchapter explores the various ways in which the base has provided assistance to those seeking political change in Cuba.

During the early years of the base's establishment, the United States actively supported anti-Castro groups, providing them with training, intelligence, and resources. These efforts were aimed at destabilizing the Cuban government and promoting democratic values on the island. Diplomats and historians will find this section particularly interesting as it sheds light on the covert operations conducted by the U.S. government during the Cold War era.

The base's strategic location and infrastructure have also made it a key hub for intelligence gathering and counterterrorism efforts. The United States has used Guantanamo to monitor and disrupt activities of groups such as the Revolutionary Armed Forces of Cuba (FARC) and the National Liberation Army (ELN). By sharing information with Cuban dissidents and opposition groups, the base has facilitated their efforts to expose human rights abuses and promote democratic ideals.

Furthermore, Guantanamo has played a vital role in refugee processing and migration control. In times of political instability, Cubans seeking asylum have found refuge within the base's borders. Diplomats and historians will be intrigued to learn about the challenges faced in handling large influxes of migrants and the legal and political controversies surrounding their presence.

The support provided by the Guantanamo Naval Base to Cuban dissidents and opposition groups has not been without its critics. Some argue that the base's involvement in covert operations and intelligence gathering compromises its credibility as a promoter of democracy and human rights. Others question the legality of these actions under international law.

As U.S.-Cuba relations continue to evolve, the future of the Guantanamo Naval Base remains uncertain. Diplomats and historians will be keen to explore the potential impact its closure or continued operation may have on efforts to promote democracy and stability in Cuba. Understanding the historical context and significance of the base's support to Cuban dissidents and opposition groups is crucial in assessing its future role in U.S.-Cuba relations.

In conclusion, the support provided by the Guantanamo Naval Base to Cuban dissidents and opposition groups has been a crucial aspect of its history. This subchapter delves into the covert operations, intelligence gathering efforts, refugee processing, and migration control activities that have shaped the base's contribution to political change in Cuba. Diplomats and historians will find a wealth of information here, shedding light on the complexities of the U.S.-Cuba relationship and the base's role in promoting democracy and human rights.

The impact on U.S.-Cuba relations and the Cuban government's response

The U.S.-Cuba relations have been greatly influenced by the presence of the Guantanamo Naval Base. Since its establishment in 1903, the base has played a crucial role in shaping the dynamics between the two countries. This subchapter will delve into the various impacts of the base on U.S.-Cuba relations and how the Cuban government has responded to its presence.

Throughout history, the Guantanamo Naval Base has been a symbol of American imperialism in Cuba. Its establishment during the early 20th century marked a significant shift in the power dynamics between the two nations. The base became a constant reminder of Cuba's limited sovereignty, as it was leased to the United States under the Platt Amendment. This arrangement greatly strained U.S.-Cuba relations, leading to resentment and anti-American sentiments among the Cuban population.

The Spanish-American War further exacerbated tensions between the two countries. The Guantanamo Naval Base played a pivotal role during the war, providing a strategic location for the U.S. forces. Its significance in the conflict solidified its role as a symbol of U.S. dominance in Cuba.

During the Cold War, the Guantanamo Naval Base became even more significant. It served as a crucial listening post for monitoring Soviet activities in the Caribbean region. This heightened the already strained relations between the United States and Cuba, as the base was seen as a tool for American espionage and intelligence gathering.

The Cuban government has consistently voiced its opposition to the presence of the Guantanamo Naval Base. Fidel Castro, in particular, made it a point to denounce the base as a violation of Cuban sovereignty. The Cuban government has called for the removal of the base and the return of the territory to Cuba.

The legal and political controversies surrounding the Guantanamo Naval Base have added fuel to the fire. The detention center that was established at the base in the aftermath of the 9/11 attacks sparked international outrage and condemned the United States for human rights violations. The Cuban government has been vocal in its criticism of the detention center and its treatment of prisoners.

The economic impact of the Guantanamo Naval Base on the local Cuban community has been mixed. While it has provided some employment opportunities, the base has also created a sense of dependency on the United States. The Cuban government has criticized this reliance on the base and has called for the diversification of the local economy.

Looking towards the future, the fate of the Guantanamo Naval Base remains uncertain. Its potential impact on U.S.-Cuba relations cannot be underestimated. Any decision regarding the base's future will have far-reaching consequences for the diplomatic ties between the two nations.

In conclusion, the presence of the Guantanamo Naval Base has had a profound impact on U.S.-Cuba relations. It has served as a symbol of American imperialism, strained diplomatic ties, and sparked legal and political controversies. The Cuban government has consistently opposed the base and its actions. As diplomats and historians, it is vital to understand the complexities surrounding the base and its role in shaping U.S.-Cuba relations throughout history.

The Challenges and Limitations of U.S. Democracy Promotion through the Naval Base

Introduction:

The Guantanamo Naval Base in Cuba has played a significant role in the history of U.S.-Cuba relations. Throughout its existence, the base has been associated with various legal, political, and economic controversies. One area where the base has faced considerable challenges is in the U.S. efforts to promote democracy and stability in Cuba. This subchapter will explore the limitations and difficulties encountered in this endeavor.

Historical Background:

To understand the challenges, it is important to trace the establishment and early history of the Guantanamo Naval Base. Built during the Spanish-American War, the base has always been seen as a symbol of U.S. military presence in the region. Its significance in the Cold War further solidified its importance. However, this historical context has also created obstacles in promoting democracy as it has been perceived by many Cubans as an intrusion on their sovereignty.

Legal and Political Controversies:

The legal and political controversies surrounding the base have made democracy promotion a complex task. The indefinite detention of individuals in Guantanamo Bay and the use of enhanced interrogation techniques have raised questions about human rights and international law. These controversies have undermined the credibility of the U.S. in its efforts to promote democratic values.

Economic Impact and Local Community:

The economic impact of the base on the local Cuban community has been another challenge. While the base has provided employment opportunities, it has also created a sense of dependency on the U.S. This dependence can hinder the development of a self-sustaining democratic society in Cuba.

Role in Intelligence Gathering and Counterterrorism:

The Guantanamo Naval Base has been instrumental in intelligence gathering and counterterrorism efforts. However, this role has also raised concerns regarding the violation of human rights and international law. The base's association with controversial practices has made it difficult for the U.S. to effectively promote democracy while maintaining its security interests.

Conclusion:

The challenges and limitations faced by the U.S. in promoting democracy through the Guantanamo Naval Base are multifaceted. Historical controversies, legal and political issues, economic dependencies, and concerns over human rights have all contributed to the difficulty of this endeavor. As diplomats and historians, it is crucial to critically examine these challenges and explore alternative approaches that can foster democracy and stability in Cuba without compromising fundamental values. The future of the Guantanamo Naval Base will undoubtedly have a significant impact on U.S.-Cuba relations, and finding a balance between security interests and democratic promotion will require thoughtful consideration and collaboration between both nations.

The Cuban government's resistance to U.S. influence and democracy promotion

Throughout history, the Cuban government has displayed a steadfast resistance to U.S. influence and democracy promotion. This subchapter delves into the complex dynamics between the United States and Cuba, shedding light on the reasons behind Cuba's resistance and its implications for U.S.-Cuba relations.

From the early days of the U.S. Naval Base in Guantanamo Bay, Cuba, the Cuban government has viewed it as a symbol of U.S. imperialism and a violation of its sovereignty. The base's establishment and early history were marked by tensions, with the Cuban government expressing its strong opposition to the presence of a foreign military base on its territory. This resistance was further fueled by the base's role in the Spanish-American War, which solidified the perception that the United States was using Cuba as a pawn in its global power games.

The Cold War era intensified Cuba's resistance to U.S. influence, as the Guantanamo Naval Base became a significant strategic location for U.S. operations in the region. The Cuban government, led by Fidel Castro, saw the base as a symbol of U.S. aggression and a constant threat to its socialist ideals. This resistance culminated in the Cuban Missile Crisis, when the United States discovered Soviet missiles in Cuba, triggering a standoff that brought the world to the brink of nuclear war.

The legal and political controversies surrounding the Guantanamo Naval Base have further strained U.S.-Cuba relations. The indefinite detention of individuals at the base, without trial or access to legal representation, has been a source of international criticism and a violation of human rights. The Cuban government has vehemently opposed these practices and has called for the base's closure.

In addition to its symbolic significance, the Guantanamo Naval Base has had an economic impact on the local Cuban community. While the base has provided some employment opportunities, it has also contributed to a sense of resentment among the Cuban people, who view it as a reminder of U.S. dominance and economic inequality.

The resistance of the Cuban government to U.S. influence and democracy promotion has had far-reaching consequences. It has hindered U.S. efforts to promote democracy and stability in Cuba, as the Cuban government views these initiatives as a form of interference and regime change attempts. Furthermore, the Guantanamo Naval Base has complicated U.S. refugee processing and migration control efforts, as it has served as a point of contention between the two nations.

Looking towards the future, the fate of the Guantanamo Naval Base remains uncertain. Its potential impact on U.S.-Cuba relations cannot be ignored, as it continues to be a symbol of the deeply rooted tensions between the two nations. Resolving these issues will require open dialogue and a willingness to address historical grievances, with the ultimate goal of fostering mutual understanding and cooperation.

The limitations imposed by the legal and political controversies surrounding the base

The limitations imposed by the legal and political controversies surrounding the base have had a profound impact on the history of the U.S. Naval Base in Guantanamo, Cuba, and its importance in U.S.-Cuba relations. For diplomats and historians seeking to understand the complex dynamics at play, it is crucial to delve into the legal and political intricacies that have shaped the base's past and continue to influence its future.

One of the main limitations stems from the legal disputes surrounding the base's presence on Cuban soil. Since its establishment in 1903, the U.S. has maintained a lease agreement with Cuba, granting it exclusive control over the territory. However, this arrangement has been a source of contention, with Cuba arguing that the lease is illegal and should be terminated. This has created an ongoing legal challenge for both nations, impeding any long-term strategic planning for the base.

Moreover, the base has become a political lightning rod, particularly in the context of U.S.-Cuba relations. The Cuban government views the base as a symbol of U.S. imperialism and a constant reminder of the troubled history between the two nations. This perception has fueled anti-American sentiment and shaped Cuba's diplomatic strategy, making any progress in bilateral relations contingent upon resolving the base's status.

Additionally, the base's controversial use as a detention facility has significantly impacted its standing in the international community. The detention of suspected terrorists and the human rights concerns associated with their treatment have led to widespread condemnation. This has further complicated diplomatic efforts, as the base's association with human rights violations has eroded its credibility and hindered potential partnerships.

The political controversies surrounding the base have also influenced the U.S.'s ability to fully utilize it for strategic purposes. The uncertain future of the base has made it difficult for the U.S. to invest in long-term infrastructure, limiting its operational capabilities. Furthermore, the political sensitivities surrounding the base have restricted the U.S.'s ability to engage in open dialogue with Cuba, hindering the potential for cooperation on shared security concerns.

In conclusion, the legal and political controversies surrounding the U.S. Naval Base in Guantanamo have imposed significant limitations on its historical trajectory and its importance in U.S.-Cuba relations. The ongoing legal disputes, political animosities, and human rights concerns have hindered strategic planning, diplomatic progress, and operational capabilities. For diplomats and historians studying the base's history and its impact on U.S.-Cuba relations, understanding these limitations is crucial to grasping the complex dynamics at play and exploring potential avenues for resolution.

The effectiveness of democracy promotion efforts in Cuba through Guantanamo Bay

The Guantanamo Naval Base has played a significant role in U.S.-Cuba relations throughout history. While primarily known for its association with the controversial detention center, it has also been a platform for democracy promotion efforts in Cuba. This subchapter will delve into the effectiveness of these initiatives and their impact on the local Cuban community.

Guantanamo Bay has served as a symbolic representation of American values and democratic principles in Cuba. Diplomats and historians will find it intriguing to examine the various initiatives undertaken by the United States to promote democracy and stability in Cuba through this strategic base.

Despite political and legal controversies surrounding the Guantanamo Naval Base, it has been utilized as a tool to support democratic values. The United States has implemented programs to foster civil society, human rights, and political participation in Cuba. These efforts have included educational exchanges, cultural programs, and the provision of resources to local organizations advocating for democratic reforms.

However, the effectiveness of these democracy promotion initiatives remains a subject of debate. Critics argue that the impact has been limited due to the strained U.S.-Cuba relations and the Cuban government's resistance to democratic reforms. Others contend that these efforts have opened channels of communication and raised awareness about democratic principles among the Cuban population.

Moreover, the economic impact of the Guantanamo Naval Base on the local Cuban community cannot be overlooked. The base has provided employment opportunities and economic stability to the region. This subchapter will explore whether these economic benefits have contributed to the promotion of democratic values in Cuba or if they have perpetuated a dependence on the United States.

To fully grasp the significance of democracy promotion through Guantanamo Bay, it is crucial to analyze the base's role in intelligence gathering and counterterrorism efforts. By understanding the complex interplay between security concerns and democratic aspirations, diplomats and historians can gain a comprehensive understanding of the effectiveness of these initiatives.

Ultimately, this subchapter will aim to shed light on the successes and challenges faced in the United States' efforts to promote democracy in Cuba through the Guantanamo Naval Base. It will provide insights into the intricate relationship between the base, U.S.-Cuba relations, human rights, and the future of democracy promotion in the region.

Chapter 7: The Role of the Guantanamo Naval Base in Refugee Processing and Migration Control

The Naval Base as a Center for Refugee Processing

Throughout its history, the Guantanamo Naval Base in Cuba has played a significant role in various aspects of U.S.-Cuba relations. One of its lesser-known functions is its role as a center for refugee processing and migration control. This subchapter will explore the importance of the base in managing refugee flows and its impact on both the United States and Cuba.

During the Cold War, the Guantanamo Naval Base served as a vital facility for processing refugees fleeing from communist regimes in Cuba and other parts of the world. The base provided a safe haven for those seeking refuge, ensuring their safety and security until they could be processed and resettled in the United States or other countries. This humanitarian role of the base showcased the United States' commitment to providing assistance to those in need, while also serving as a symbolic gesture of support for democracy and freedom.

The Guantanamo Naval Base's location and infrastructure made it an ideal center for refugee processing. Its proximity to Cuba allowed for quick and efficient transportation of refugees to the base, while its facilities were well-equipped to accommodate and process large numbers of individuals. Moreover, the base's secure environment ensured the safety of both refugees and personnel involved in the processing operations.

The base's role in refugee processing has not been without controversy, however. In recent years, the detention of suspected terrorists at Guantanamo Bay has overshadowed its humanitarian function. The treatment of detainees and the legal and ethical questions surrounding their detention have raised concerns about human rights and international law. The ongoing debate over the future of the base and its potential impact on U.S.-Cuba relations remains a contentious issue.

Despite these controversies, the Guantanamo Naval Base's legacy as a center for refugee processing is an important part of its history. It demonstrates the base's versatility and its ability to adapt to changing geopolitical circumstances. The base's commitment to providing assistance to those in need has been a testament to the United States' values and humanitarian principles.

As diplomats and historians, it is crucial to understand the multifaceted role of the Guantanamo Naval Base in U.S.-Cuba relations. Examining its function as a center for refugee processing sheds light on the complex dynamics between the two nations and the broader international community. By delving into this topic, we can gain a deeper understanding of the base's historical significance and its potential impact on the future of U.S.-Cuba relations.

The history of refugee processing at Guantanamo Bay

Since its establishment in 1903, the U.S. Naval Base in Guantanamo Bay, Cuba, has played a significant role in various aspects of U.S.-Cuba relations. One such aspect is the base's involvement in refugee processing and migration control. Over the years, Guantanamo Bay has served as a temporary home for thousands of individuals fleeing persecution, political unrest, and economic hardship in their home countries.

During the early years of the base, the United States utilized Guantanamo Bay as a processing center for refugees from the Caribbean and Central America. This practice gained momentum during the Spanish-American War, when the base became a key location for processing Cuban refugees seeking asylum in the United States. The influx of Cuban refugees and the establishment of refugee camps at Guantanamo Bay marked a turning point in the history of the base, making it an important site for migration control.

The Cold War era further highlighted the significance of Guantanamo Bay in refugee processing. As political tensions between the United States and Cuba intensified, the base became a destination for individuals escaping the communist regime. Thousands of Cuban refugees, known as balseros, were intercepted at sea by the U.S. Coast Guard and transported to Guantanamo Bay for processing. The base served as a temporary shelter for these refugees while their cases were reviewed, and many were eventually resettled in the United States.

However, the refugee processing at Guantanamo Bay has not been without controversy. Human rights organizations and international bodies have raised concerns about the treatment of refugees at the base, particularly during the early years of its operation. Reports of inadequate living conditions, limited access to legal representation, and violations of human rights have sparked debates about the base's compliance with international law.

In recent years, the role of Guantanamo Bay in refugee processing has diminished. The base has shifted its focus primarily to detainment facilities for individuals suspected of terrorism, overshadowing its historical role as a processing center for refugees. Nevertheless, the legacy of Guantanamo Bay as a place of refuge for those fleeing persecution remains a significant part of its history.

As diplomats and historians delve into the history of the U.S. Naval Base in Guantanamo Bay, it is essential to explore its role in refugee processing and migration control. By understanding this aspect, we gain insight into the base's humanitarian undertakings, the challenges it has faced, and its broader impact on U.S.-Cuba relations. As the future of Guantanamo Bay continues to evolve, it is important to reflect on the lessons learned from its history and consider its potential impact on the ongoing quest for democracy and stability in Cuba.

The challenges and successes in processing refugees

The Guantanamo Naval Base has played a crucial role in refugee processing and migration control, serving as a key point of entry for individuals fleeing persecution and seeking asylum in the United States. Over the years, this process has been marked by both challenges and successes, reflecting the complex nature of dealing with refugee populations in a highly sensitive and politically charged environment.

One of the primary challenges faced in processing refugees at Guantanamo has been the sheer volume of individuals seeking asylum. Throughout its history, the base has witnessed waves of refugees from different regions, including Haitians, Cubans, and individuals from other Caribbean countries. Managing and accommodating such large numbers of people has put a strain on the resources and infrastructure of the base, leading to overcrowding and logistical difficulties.

Another significant challenge has been ensuring the safety and security of the refugees while their cases are being processed. The Guantanamo Naval Base has had to establish robust screening procedures to identify potential security threats and prevent the entry of individuals with criminal backgrounds or links to terrorist organizations. This has required close coordination with various intelligence agencies and law enforcement entities, adding another layer of complexity to the refugee processing system.

Despite these challenges, there have been notable successes in processing refugees at Guantanamo. The base has been instrumental in providing a safe haven for those fleeing persecution and violence in their home countries. By offering temporary shelter and access to basic necessities such as food, healthcare, and education, the base has been able to provide a lifeline for refugees during their transition period.

Moreover, the Guantanamo Naval Base has also played a crucial role in facilitating the resettlement of refugees in the United States. Working closely with international organizations, such as the United Nations High Commissioner for Refugees (UNHCR) and non-governmental organizations, the base has been able to identify eligible refugees and expedite their transfer to the mainland for permanent resettlement.

In recent years, however, the refugee processing system at Guantanamo has faced criticism and controversy. Concerns have been raised regarding the treatment and conditions of refugees, with allegations of human rights abuses and violations of international law. These controversies have prompted calls for reform and greater transparency in the refugee processing procedures at the base.

Looking to the future, the Guantanamo Naval Base will continue to play a significant role in refugee processing and migration control. As global displacement crises persist, the base's capacity to provide a safe haven and facilitate the resettlement of refugees will remain vital. However, it is crucial that efforts are made to address the challenges and controversies surrounding the base's refugee processing system, ensuring that the rights and well-being of refugees are protected, and international obligations are upheld. By finding a balance between security concerns and humanitarian considerations, the Guantanamo Naval Base can continue to contribute positively to U.S.-Cuba relations and the broader global refugee crisis.

The impact on U.S.-Cuba relations and regional migration dynamics

Throughout its history, the U.S. Naval Base in Guantanamo Bay, Cuba, has played a significant role in shaping U.S.-Cuba relations and regional migration dynamics. This subchapter will delve into the various ways in which the base has influenced these aspects, providing a comprehensive understanding for diplomats and historians alike.

The establishment and early history of the U.S. Naval Base in Guantanamo Bay set the stage for future interactions between the United States and Cuba. Initially acquired during the Spanish-American War, the base became a symbol of U.S. military presence and exertion of influence in the region. Its strategic location and proximity to Cuba made it a vital asset for the United States, solidifying its role in U.S.-Cuba relations.

During the Cold War, the Guantanamo Naval Base gained even greater significance. Its proximity to the communist regime in Cuba made it a focal point of tension and conflict. The base became a hub for intelligence gathering and counterterrorism efforts, as the United States sought to monitor and counteract any potential threats from Cuba. This further strained U.S.-Cuba relations, creating a contentious atmosphere that lasted for decades.

The legal and political controversies surrounding the Guantanamo Naval Base have also had a lasting impact on U.S.-Cuba relations. The base's status as a territory leased by the United States has been a source of contention, with Cuba arguing for its return. The detention center established at Guantanamo Bay, which housed suspected terrorists, further added to the controversy and strained relations between the two countries.

The economic impact of the Guantanamo Naval Base on the local Cuban community cannot be overlooked. The base has provided employment opportunities and economic stability for many Cubans, serving as a major source of income. However, this economic reliance also highlights the complex relationship between the base and the surrounding community, as well as the potential consequences of any changes to the base's operations.

Moreover, the Guantanamo Naval Base has played a crucial role in refugee processing and migration control. Over the years, it has been used as a holding facility for refugees attempting to reach the United States. This has not only affected regional migration dynamics but has also raised questions about human rights and international law.

Looking towards the future, the fate of the Guantanamo Naval Base will undoubtedly impact U.S.-Cuba relations. As diplomatic efforts continue to normalize relations between the two countries, the base's future remains uncertain. Its potential closure or transformation could significantly alter the dynamics between the United States and Cuba, opening new possibilities for collaboration or further straining relations.

In conclusion, the U.S. Naval Base in Guantanamo Bay has had a profound impact on U.S.-Cuba relations and regional migration dynamics. From its establishment to its role during the Cold War, the base has shaped the relationship between the two countries in various ways. The legal controversies, economic impact, and role in intelligence gathering and migration control have all contributed to the complex nature of this relationship. As the future of the base remains uncertain, it is crucial to examine its potential impact on the future of U.S.-Cuba relations.

Migration Control Efforts and the Naval Base

The Guantanamo Naval Base has played a significant role in refugee processing and migration control throughout its history. This chapter delves into the efforts made by the base in managing the influx of migrants and its impact on U.S.-Cuba relations.

Since its establishment in 1903, the Guantanamo Naval Base has served as a strategic location for the United States. Over the years, it has become a vital point of entry for migrants seeking refuge or attempting to reach American shores. The base has seen waves of migrants from various regions, including Haiti, Cuba, and other Caribbean nations.

During times of political instability or economic crises in the region, the Guantanamo Naval Base has been at the forefront of managing migration flows. It has provided a secure location for processing refugees, ensuring their safety and well-being before further actions are taken. The base has served as a temporary home for thousands of migrants, offering them shelter, medical assistance, and humanitarian aid.

The migration control efforts of the base have not been without controversy. The United States has faced criticism from human rights organizations and international bodies for its handling of migrants at Guantanamo. The detention of individuals, particularly during the War on Terror, has raised concerns about the base's compliance with international law and the treatment of detainees.

However, it is important to recognize that the Guantanamo Naval Base has also played a crucial role in preventing illegal migration and combating human trafficking. The base's proximity to the Caribbean region has allowed for effective interception and prevention of unauthorized entry into the United States. The efforts of the base have contributed to maintaining stability and security in the region.

Looking ahead, the future of the Guantanamo Naval Base and its impact on U.S.-Cuba relations remain uncertain. The shifting political landscape and the ongoing normalization of relations between the two countries have raised questions about the base's continued existence. The potential closure or reconfiguration of the base could have far-reaching implications for migration control efforts, U.S.-Cuba relations, and the local Cuban community.

In conclusion, the Guantanamo Naval Base has been a key player in managing migration flows and controlling unauthorized entries. Its role in refugee processing and migration control has had significant implications for U.S.-Cuba relations. As the future of the base remains uncertain, it is crucial for diplomats and historians to analyze and understand the impact it has had on migration, human rights, and international law.

The role of the naval base in intercepting and deterring migration attempts

The Guantanamo Naval Base has played a significant role in controlling migration attempts from Cuba to the United States. This subchapter aims to explore the intricacies of this role and its implications on both U.S.-Cuba relations and international law.

Since its establishment, the naval base has been strategically located to intercept and deter migrants attempting to cross the treacherous waters between Cuba and the United States. The base's proximity to the Windward Passage, a key migratory route, has made it an ideal spot for monitoring and responding to migration attempts. Diplomats and historians would find it intriguing to understand the operational mechanisms employed by the naval base in these efforts.

Throughout its history, the naval base has witnessed various waves of migration, including the Cuban Balsero Crisis in the 1990s. During this period, the base played a crucial role in rescuing and processing thousands of Cuban migrants attempting to reach American shores. Understanding the logistical challenges faced by the naval base in handling such large-scale migration operations would provide valuable insights into the complexities of this issue.

Moreover, this subchapter would delve into the legal and political controversies surrounding the naval base's involvement in migration control. The base has been criticized for its treatment of migrants and the detainment of individuals in Guantanamo Bay. The discussions would explore the impact of these controversies on human rights and international law, as well as the implications for U.S.-Cuba relations.

Additionally, this subchapter would examine the future of the naval base in relation to migration control. With changing political dynamics between the United States and Cuba, it is essential to analyze the potential impact of any modifications to the base's operations on migration patterns and U.S.-Cuba relations. This analysis would require a careful assessment of diplomatic and historical perspectives.

Overall, diplomats and historians interested in the U.S.-Cuba relationship and the history of the Guantanamo Naval Base would find this subchapter insightful. By exploring the role of the base in intercepting and deterring migration attempts, the book aims to provide a comprehensive understanding of the complexities surrounding this crucial aspect of the naval base's operations.

The cooperation between the U.S. and Cuba

The cooperation between the U.S. and Cuba has been a complex and contentious issue throughout history. In the context of the Guantanamo Naval Base, this cooperation has taken on various dimensions and has influenced the relationships between the two countries in significant ways.

The establishment and early history of the U.S. Naval Base in Guantanamo Bay, Cuba, marked the beginning of this cooperation. The base was established in 1903, following the signing of the Cuban-American Treaty, which granted the United States a lease for the land. This marked the first step in a long and intricate relationship between the two nations.

During the Spanish-American War, the Guantanamo Naval Base played a crucial role in the conflict. It served as a strategic location for the U.S. Navy, allowing them to monitor and control the waters surrounding Cuba. This involvement in the war had a lasting impact on U.S.-Cuba relations, shaping the power dynamics between the two countries.

The Cold War further intensified the significance of the Guantanamo Naval Base. As tensions between the United States and Cuba escalated, the base became a focal point for both sides. It served as a surveillance and intelligence gathering center for the U.S., providing crucial information during the Cold War era. The base's role in this period had profound implications for U.S.-Cuba relations, as it highlighted the ideological divide between the two nations.

The legal and political controversies surrounding the Guantanamo Naval Base have also shaped the cooperative efforts between the U.S. and Cuba. The base has been the subject of intense debate, particularly regarding issues of human rights and international law. The detention center established at Guantanamo Bay in the aftermath of the September 11 attacks further complicated the relationship, as it became a symbol of the United States' controversial approach to counterterrorism.

The economic impact of the Guantanamo Naval Base on the local Cuban community cannot be overlooked. The base has provided employment opportunities and economic benefits to the surrounding area, contributing to the local economy and shaping the livelihoods of the Cuban people. This economic cooperation has had both positive and negative implications, influencing the perceptions and attitudes of the local population.

Looking towards the future, the fate of the Guantanamo Naval Base remains uncertain. Its potential impact on U.S.-Cuba relations cannot be underestimated. As diplomatic efforts between the two countries continue to evolve, the future of the base will undoubtedly play a significant role in shaping the overall relationship between the U.S. and Cuba.

In conclusion, the cooperation between the U.S. and Cuba regarding the Guantanamo Naval Base has spanned over a century and has had a profound impact on their relations. From its establishment to its role in historical events, controversies, economic implications, and its future outlook, the base has been a key factor in shaping the complex and multifaceted relationship between these two nations. Diplomats and historians must delve into the intricacies of this cooperation to gain a comprehensive understanding of the history and significance of the Guantanamo Naval Base in U.S.-Cuba relations.